30 Day Whole Foods Challenge

Irresistible Whole Food Recipes For Your Healthy Lifestyle - Lose Weight, Boost Your Metabolism, and Prevent Disease

© **Copyright 2017 - All rights reserved.**

The contents of this book may not be reproduced, duplicated or transmitted without direct written permission from the author.

Under no circumstances will any legal responsibility or blame be held against the publisher for any reparation, damages, or monetary loss due to the information herein, either directly or indirectly.

Legal Notice:

This book is copyright protected. This is only for personal use. You cannot amend, distribute, sell, use, quote or paraphrase any part or the content within this book without the consent of the author.

Disclaimer Notice:

Please note the information contained within this document is for educational and entertainment purposes only. Every attempt has been made to provide accurate, up to date and reliable complete information. No warranties of any kind are expressed or implied. Readers acknowledge that the author is not engaging in the rendering of legal, financial, medical or professional advice. The content of this book has been derived from various sources. Please consult a licensed professional before attempting any techniques outlined in this book.

By reading this document, the reader agrees that under no circumstances are is the author responsible for any losses, direct or indirect, which are incurred as a result of the use of information contained within this document, including, but not limited to, — errors, omissions, or inaccuracies.

Table of Contents

CHAPTER 1: WHAT IS THE WHOLE FOOD 30 DAY CHALLENGE 4

CHAPTER 2: WHAT ARE THE BENEFITS? 4

Intentional Living 5

Knowledge 6

Sugar 7

Grains 8

Dairy 8

Legumes 8

CHAPTER 3: YES & NO FOODS 8

30 Day Whole Foods Challenge 9

Rules for the 30 Day Whole Foods Challenge 9

A Quick Yes & No Whole Food Challenge Chart 10

CHAPTER 4: WHY COMMUNITY IS IMPORTANT 11

CHAPTER 5: HOW TO REINTRODUCE FOODS TO YOUR DIET 12

CHAPTER 6: GROCERY LISTS 13

Essentials to Stock Your Pantry Grocery List 13

Meal Plan Grocery List 14
    Week 1 (and again on week 3) 14
    Week 2 (and again on week 4) 18
    Holiday Meal Grocery List 21

CHAPTER 7: 30 DAY MEAL PLAN 22
    Week 1 & 3 22
    Week 2 & 4 23

CHAPTER 8: SNACKS — 25

CHAPTER 9: RECIPES — 27

Breakfast (Week 1 & 3) — 27
- Kale & Sweet Potato Hash — 27
- Avocado & Egg — 28
- Beet Berry Bowl — 28
- Banana Almond Smoothie — 29
- Roasted Veggie Breakfast Bowl with Fried Egg — 30
- Loaded Breakfast Potatoes — 32
- Pumpkin Pudding — 33

Lunch (Week 1 & 3) — 34
- Chicken & Zucchini Poppers — 34
- Grilled Pineapple Chicken — 35
- Citrus Shrimp Salad with Fruit — 36
- Thai-Style Coconut Chicken Soup — 37
- Roasted Citrus And Herb Chicken Recipe — 39
- Artichoke & Tomato Salad — 40
- Chicken and Summer Squash Sauté — 41

Dinner (Week 1 & 3) — 41
- Chiptole Lime Chicken — 42
- Roast Turkey with Root Vegetables — 43
- Mint Lamb Chops — 44
- Hasselback Potatoes — 45
- Balsamic Flank Steak with Mushrooms — 46
- Balsamic Mushrooms — 47
- Lemon Tilapia with Asparagus — 47
- Citrus Shrimp & Steak — 49
- Spicy Pork Tenderloin & Collard Greens — 50

Breakfast (Week 2 & 4) — 51
- Zucchini Cakes with Fried Egg — 51
- Veggie Bacon Egg Scramble — 52
- Breakfast Salad — 53
- Breakfast Casserole — 54
- Kale and Strawberry Smoothie — 56
- Pork and Broccoli Slaw Frittata — 56
- Spinach Tomato Omelet — 57

Lunch (Week 2 & 4) — 58
- Garlic Ginger Chicken — 58
- Curry Coconut Cauliflower Soup — 59
- Bacon Wrapped Coconut Chicken Nuggets — 61

    Artichoke Chicken Thighs … 62
    Meatballs … 63
    Tomato Basil Beef Soup … 63
    Buffalo Wings with Veggies … 64

Dinner (Week 2 & 4) … 65
    Sautéed Cabbage and Potatoes … 66
    Salmon with Prosciutto Wrapped Asparagus … 67
    Prosciutto Wrapped Asparagus … 67
    Chicken and Roasted Veggies … 68
    Pumpkin Chili … 69
    Loaded Baked Potatoes … 71
    Spicy Beef and Broccoli … 72
    Pulled Pork Shoulder with Turnips … 73

CHAPTER 10: HOLIDAY TIPS & ENCOURAGEMENT … 74
    Caramelized Brussel Sprouts / Sweet Potato Casserole / Stuffing / Pumpkin Butter Biscuit / Cranberry Sauce … 76

CHAPTER 11: HOLIDAY SIDE DISHES … 76
    Caramelized Brussel Sprouts … 76
    Sweet Potato Casserole … 77
    Stuffing … 78
    Pumpkin Butter Biscuit … 79
    Cranberry Sauce … 79

CHAPTER 12: YOU DID IT! … 80

CHAPTER 13: MEASUREMENTS & EQUIVALENTS … 81

CHAPTER 14: UK TO US CONVERSIONS … 81

Chapter 1: What is the Whole Food 30 Day Challenge

Have you ever craved a reset button on your life? Do you struggle with low energy, skin issues, chronic pain, or unexplainable aches and pains? Are you willing to give 30 days to reset your body, feel energized, and finally discover what it is that is causing these symptoms?

If you've answered yes, sports nutritionist David Hartwig and his wife Melissa created the Whole30 to combat these symptoms. Simply put, the Whole Food 30 Day Challenge is a clean eating reset that changes your relationship to food. It breaks psychological habits and detoxes your body from food group culprits. This isn't a weight-loss diet (though weight-loss is a common side effect) or a fad. Testimonials back it up as a training tool to rethink and reevaluate our relationship with food. It's a strict form of Paleo that breaks food addictions and sets you up for individual lifestyle changes.

By setting aside 30 consecutive days to eat healthy clean foods you will begin to discover the individual needs of your body. This elimination meal plan cuts out common food groups that induce craving, are gut damaging, inflammatory, and disrupting to blood sugar. Sugar, grains, dairy and legumes can have a potentially harming effect on your body without you even knowing it.

For 30 days you will eat real food. Every meal will include ingredients you can pronounce. Moderate portions of protein combined with lots of vegetables, a few fruits and plenty of natural fats reset your palate to crave healthy nutritious meals again. Whole food 30 is about making clean food choices. It is not about calorie counting, measuring or weighing yourself. It is about eating well and fueling your body.

Habits are never easy to break but with proper preparation and commitment your relationship with food and overall health will change.

Think of Whole 30 as a 30-day experiment into the most important topic: YOU.

It's 30 days. What do you have to lose?

Chapter 2: What Are The Benefits?

Scientific data and testimonials back up the claims of the Whole30 food challenge. While Whole30 has not been scientifically analyzed, the decisions of what to eliminate and what to allow come from careful nutritional study. Think of this challenge as an intense version of Paleo for 30 whole days.

The purpose of this challenge is to reset your body so that you can begin tailoring your diet to individual needs. The right food choices may not be the right ones for someone else. The purpose of elimination diets is to learn what is right for you. Whole30 is not a one size fits all because one size never actually fits.

By removing possible toxins from your diet your body has time to heal. Once 30 days have been completed you will begin reintroducing these food groups to your diet until you discover which or if any are the culprit. Added benefits of this challenge include intentionality in food choices, increased knowledge of ingredients, a new relationship with food, higher energy and testimonials of healing.

Intentional Living

Intentionality in food choices comes from discipline. Success is rarely achieved with out a clear goal and action plan. Eliminating even one ingredient or food group from your diet requires attention. Labels must be read. Recipes need to be planned. A last minute fast food run or trip to the grocery store to decide on dinner moments before will sabotage your end goals.

This book that you hold in your hand, or on your screen, is a tool to help you intentionally map out the 30 days ahead. In addition to maintaining your health goals the stress of what's for dinner, lunch, and breakfast has now been mapped out for you. Be intentional in your daily life to reduce stress and increase health. This advice isn't just for a menu, but in how you interact with the world at large. Stressors take us by surprise, when the controllable parts of life are already handled it frees us up to give our attention fully to the problem at hand.

The mind is powerful. What we think is possible. When we believe we will fail, we do. There are no easy solutions to health but instead paths that lead us to a healthier tomorrow. This is one of those paths.

To set ourselves up for success it is important to create a game plan. Focusing on the restrictiveness of Whole30 sets us up for failure. When you focus on what you cannot have it becomes forefront in your mind and the cravings become consuming. Self-doubt is a self-fulfilling prophecy.

Focusing on the positive encourages us forward. When we possess this mindset and misstep along the way it strengthens determination. The failure is not defeat but only a challenge along the road to success. When we succeed, our reaction is "I knew I could!"

Self-imposed limitations must be overcome to reach health goals. That's where this book steps in. By creating a 30-day meal plan with delicious recipes, a detailed shopping list, instructions for one full prep day, along with freezing and serving details, it is our hope to eliminate the frustration and create ease and fulfillment at dinnertime. This won't be about what you're leaving out, instead let's focus on what you will be gaining.

Be intentional with your goals. If you cannot get behind your dream of living healthier how will you get others to take you serious? Picture yourself celebrating! And I don't mean with cake. Picture the end; reduced pain, healthier skin, and more energy and press on towards that goal. Cast the vision not just for yourself but also for everyone around you.

Seek out the experts and learn from them. Who has already achieved what you are wanting? Bookmark testimonials of others who have completed Whole30 or print out your favorites and post them around the kitchen.

Do not let the circumstance of today wreck the direction you are headed. Complaining about the restrictions is nothing more than excuses distracting you from finding solutions to the problem. It is a lazy way to say, "Failure was not my fault." Instead see Whole30 as a solution to the problem and say, "failure is not an option."

To succeed at Whole30 you need a plan. A successful 30 days does not unintentionally happen, it takes work. You must do the work. The foundation you set out at the beginning will allow you to continue to move forward on the days you want to slip backward into self-doubt and complaint. A well-thought out plan will not allow you to fail, it will push you forward to success.

Intentional planning knows that the unpredictable will happen along the way. Don't panic when obstacles pop up: birthdays and weddings will still happen in the next 30 days, life goes on regardless of your Whole30 Challenge. Remember that every obstacle is another learning experience to put in your toolbox, an opportunity to get better and stronger.

Knowledge

Success is never handed to anyone. To succeed you must put in the work. It is the day-to-day training of your mind and habits that will lead to success. It is the one with the complaints, the one making the excuses, the one saying, "I failed because of _____", that will not complete the challenge.

Working smart and hard pays off. You have to educate yourself and know the why behind the method. Know what foods you are eliminating and the reason behind them. Understanding how these foods potentially sabotage the Whole30 challenge will help you reach for a cup of tea instead of the sweet treat that you are craving.

So why are sugar, grains, dairy and legumes removed from Whole30? What is it about these common foods that are harmful? Environment and food play a key factor in harmful elements that we expose ourselves to leading to illness and disease.

Sugar

Let's talk about sugar first. Westerners like sweets. But sugar isn't just found in deserts, it's a common ingredient in processed food. Items you may not suspect (like tomato sauce, ground sausage, nut butters, etc.) are sweetened to appease our taste buds.

Before entering the bloodstream, sugar is broken down into glucose and fructose. Glucose is necessary; in fact our bodies produce it. Fructose is not necessary for our bodies and when we eat to much it is stored in the liver as fat. This can lead to non-alcoholic fatty liver disease. Overtime cells become resistant to insulin (the signal telling the cells to burn glucose instead of fat). This can lead to metabolic syndrome, cancer, obesity, cardiovascular disease, high cholesterol, and diabetes.

Empty calories lead to overconsumption of food. Sugar does not satisfy but instead leaves you feeling hungry and reaching for more food. It is highly addictive due to the dopamine dump it creates in your brain. It becomes difficult to break this addiction as you cannot abstain from food. However, with discipline and the help of the Whole30 Challenge you will abstain from added sugars. In fact, the only sugar allowed in this challenge is what is naturally found in fruit and the minuscule amount found in table salt.

As you progress through Whole30 you will be amazed by the amount of sugar we consume on a regular basis. The first time you introduce sugar back into your diet the sweetness will be overwhelming.

Grains

Wheat has been genetically engineered to withstand drought, insects and blight with chemicals. It no longer resembles the grain that our parents and grandparents baked with. It has been structurally modified in such a way that the gluten is less tolerable for our bodies and leads to a number of health concerns. It is more fattening, inflammatory, and addictive in it's modified state.

Dairy

Lactose intolerance is common. About 75 percent of the population has a difficult time digesting diary products. According to Dr. Hyman[3] dairy has been linked to prostate cancer, heart disease, and irritable bowels.

Legumes

Legumes contain phytic acid. The phytic acid restricts your body from absorbing the nutrients in the legumes and simply passes them instead. Legumes are not unhealthy, but they are not helpful when used as a substitute for other foods. The problem is they are often used to replace nutrient dense foods like meat and healthy fats.

In addition, legumes contain galaco-ligosaccharides and lectins that aggravate IBS and digestive problems. Remember, the purpose of Whole30 is to eliminate all possible causes for your symptoms and reset your body.

For those who are combating metabolic and weight issues legumes are starchy and full of carbs. There are better sources of protein available through meat and vegetables, which makes up the majority of the Whole30 diet.

Chapter 3: Yes & No Foods

The yes no list is simple. Yes to real, high-quality food and no to highly processed and common inflammatory food. Remove the grains, dairy, soy, legumes, sugar, artificial sweeteners, and alcohol.

Fill your plate with vegetables and fruit (organic when possible), meat (preferably grass-fed), eggs, seafood, and healthy fats.

Here's a more detailed list to print off and stick to the fridge for when you're reaching for a snack and need a reminder. Be sure to write down your top three reasons so they are easy to remember in your moments of weakness.

30 Day Whole Foods Challenge
RULES
- Yes to real food
- No processed foods
- No sugar, diary, legumes, grains
- No alcohol or tobacco
- Cook your own meals
- Know what you are eating

I am doing this because...
(Write your top 3 reasons for doing the 30-Day Whole Food Challenge here)
1.

2.

3.

Rules for the 30 Day Whole Foods Challenge

1. **Say YES to real food.** Shop on the perimeter of the grocery store. Read all labels and do not buy anything that you cannot pronounce or do not know what the ingredient actually is. Recognize every ingredient.

2. **Buy organic and grass-fed.** This isn't necessary because it is not feasible for everyone. However, if able it helps in eliminating pesticides and GMOs from your diet.

3. **Yes to healthy fats.** For cooking use pastured or 100% grass-fed and organic whenever possible. Cook in animal fats, clarified butter, ghee, coconut oil, and extra-virgin olive oil. Eat avocado, cashews, coconut butter, coconut meat & flakes, canned coconut milk, hazelnuts, macadamia nuts, macadamia butter, and

olives. Occasionally treat yourself to almonds, almond butter, pecans and pistachios but limit flax seeds, pine nuts, pumpkin seeds, sesame seeds, sunflower seeds, sunflower seed butter, and walnuts.

4. **Limit processed foods.** If you absolutely have to buy something from a package make sure you recognize every ingredient (see rule 1). To keep it simple do not purchase anything with more then five ingredients. When purchasing processed meats make sure that they do not have added sugar, MSG, sulfite, or carrageen.

5. **No sugar**. You will conquer your sweet tooth this month. No sugar means: no sugar or sugar substitutes, maple syrup, honey, agave, nectar, coconut sugar, date syrup, stevia, Splenda, equal, NutraSweet, xylitol, etc. If you are unsure then leave it out. If you have a sweet craving reach for a cup of tea or fresh fruit. Even dark chocolate is out, unless you're sucking down 100% cocoa.

6. **No dairy.** Use ghee or clarified butter. Do not use regular butter as it contains milk proteins and will affect results.

7. **No grains.** This includes wheat rye, barley, oats, corn, rice, millet, bulgur, sorghum, sprouted grains, and all gluten-free pseudo-cereals like quinoa, amaranth, buckwheat.

8. **Yes to "pod" legumes, no to every other legume.** This means you can eat green beans, sugar snap peas, and snow peas. You cannot have beans, soy, chickpeas, peanuts, etc.

9. **No alcohol or tobacco products.**

10. **A YES I CAN ATTITUDE.** Believe in your success from day one!

A Quick Yes & No Whole Food Challenge Chart

YES	NO
Meat (avoid processed meat)	Dairy
Seafood (Wild-caught and/or sustainable)	Sugar, sugar substitutes, honey, etc.

Eggs (pasteurized and organic)	Coffee Creamer (Even dairy & sugar free)
"Pod" legumes	Legumes
Vegetables	Peanut butter
Fruit & unsweetened fruit juice	Soy products
Dried & fresh herbs	Grain (Or substitute gluten-free products)
Salt & most spices	Spice mixes with added sugar
Nuts & seeds (Limit but don't exclude)	Carrageenan, MSG, or sulfites
Black coffee & tea	Alcohol & Tobacco
Vinegar	Ingredients you don't recognize
Coconut aminos: coconut butter, coconut meat & flakes, canned coconut milk	Junk food, or look alike junk food
Cooking fats: animal fats, clarified butter, ghee, coconut oil, and extra-virgin olive oil.	Vegetable and Peanut oil

Chapter 4: Why Community Is Important

Whom do you surround yourself with?

When beginning something as life altering as Whole30 it is important to surround yourself with people who are working toward similar goals. Are the people who are around you supportive in this endeavor or are they telling you it is useless and frustrated because it might mean small changes in their own life.

Let me tell you the truth: there will always be an area of you that needs improvement and refining. Those who tell you there is no longer room for growth do not have your best interests at heart. Whole30 is about becoming a better, healthier, more competent version of you.

Get into online communities of peers going through this program. Learn what happens along each day of the journey, how you might feel, where others struggle, and where others find success. Community is essential to success. Your mindset is essential to success. The people around you and what they are contributing, whether encouragement or distraction, will determine your success.

Sabotage comes not only from those around you. Are you sabotaging yourself with the limits you place on your own definition of you? Are you ready for this challenge? Are you comfortable where you are? If you aren't willing to push the boundaries and discover where food has a control over you, then Whole30 may not be for you, at least not yet.

The fastest way to change your confidence is to do something you normally wouldn't do. Reach outside your comfort zone and try something new. Try a new hobby. Conquer an addiction or a self-defeating thought. Do something that terrifies you and discover the euphoria of conquering that fear. You are your greatest roadblock. And only you can take the necessary steps to change. Surround yourself with like-minded people who desire better.

Life is hard and messy. Whole30 is a way to overcome obstacles, increase confidence, and improve health. It is a means to take control of your life. This program is a growth mindset. It is more then just an elimination diet but rather an evaluation to our relationship with food. It is an opportunity to hit the reset button and claim ownership of your own well being. No one else is going to do this for you. No one else's journey will look exactly like yours, and neither will their results.

Having a group of supportive individuals around you will bring you one step closer to success.

Chapter 5: How To Reintroduce Foods To Your Diet

The Whole30 is an elimination diet as well as an evaluation to our relationship with food. The goal is to remove foods from your diet to discover what may be causing you inflammation or other problems and to gain control over food rather then letting it control you. The reintroduction of foods is important. This is the experimental phase.

The last month has been about detoxing your body from what potentially harms you. Now it is time to discover which foods actually work for you and which ones work against you.

You will come off of Whole 30 slowly. After a full month of elimination, you will add one new food group to your diet every 3 to 4 days and monitor your body's reactions along the way.

I suggest getting a journal for this. On day one reintroduce legumes. On day 2 to 3 record in your journal any responses your body has. Then on day 4 introduce non-gluten grains. Monitor your body's response over day 5 and 6 recording it in your journal. On day 7 introduce glutens and record in the same manner. Over the course of two weeks you will slowly reintroduce legumes, dairy, grains, alcohol, and sugars back into your diet.

What you discover during these two weeks is the most important part of the journey. It is the why you began in the first place. Don't skip it. This is the essential step in making life style choices. Every time you do the Whole30 program you will discover something new about your body.

Figure out what your body needs and what your body needs to avoid performing at 100%. You are in complete control of your health. Knowledge is power and Whole 30 equips you to make lifestyle changes to live your best life now. You will develop a perfect specialized diet just for you. It won't look like anyone else's results because we are each unique individuals.

Don't let the food you eat steal your health and joy. Instead take control and start living a fuller healthier life today.

Chapter 6: Grocery Lists

Essentials to Stock Your Pantry Grocery List

Preparation is key to success of this diet. The more you have on hand that is compliant when hunger or cravings strike the better you will be set up for success. Meal prep and stock your pantry with easy, accessible choices. This is not an elimination diet to skimp on taste; it is an elimination diet to regain control of your life and food choices. Don't let food rule you.

Protein
- Canned protein (salmon, tuna, chicken)
- Eggs

Cooking Fats
- Animal Fats
- Clarified Butter
- Ghee
- Coconut oil
- Avocado oil

Snacks
- Macadamia Butter
- Almond Butter
- Coconut Butter
- Coconut milk and meat
- Olives
- Fresh fruits
- Raw vegetables
- Dried fruit
- Variety of nuts & seeds

Other
- Whole30 Compliant Mayonnaise
- Hot Sauce

Meal Plan Grocery List

Week 1 (and again on week 3)

A few of the ingredients on this list will come in larger containers and will keep throughout the entire month. Be sure to check your pantry before heading to the grocery store. These lists are created for a weekly shopping trip and not to stock up. Adjust as necessary.

Proteins
- Dozen eggs
- 4 slices of bacon
- ½ lb ground chicken breast
- 4 lb boneless skinless chicken breasts
- 1 ½ lb bone-in chicken pieces
- 1 (6-lb) turkey
- 5 lb flank steak
- 4 lamb chops
- 2 small pork tenderloins (about 12 oz each)
- 3 lb medium shrimp, peeled and deveined
- ¼ lb extra-large shrimp, peeled and deveined, tails removed
- 4 tilapia fillets

Fats
- 11 tbsp ghee
- 19 tbsp coconut oil
- 4 oz extra virgin olive oil
- 3 oz Avocado oil
- 35.5 oz full fat coconut milk
- ¼ cup & 1 tsp coconut cream
- 2 tbsp nut butter
- Coconut oil cooking spray

Nuts, Dried Fruit, & Seeds
- 2 tbsp pine nuts
- 1/8 cup cranberries
- Pomegranate seeds
- Coconut flakes

Pantry
- 1 tsp white wine vinegar
- 1 tbsp white wine vinegar
- 2 tbsp apple cider vinegar
- 1 cup balsamic vinaigrette
- 6 tbsp balsamic vinegar

- 2 cups cauliflower rice
- 1/8 cup coconut sugar
- 4 tbsp coconut aminos
- ¼ cup canned pumpkin puree
- 1 tsp vanilla
- 1 tbsp date paste
- 1 tsp spicy brown mustard
- 1 tbsp whole grain mustard
- ½ quart chicken stock
- Red Boat fish sauce
- ¼ jar (7 ½ oz) marinated quartered artichoke hearts
- ½ cup jarred Peppadew peppers
- Jar of Whole30 compliant chipotle

Spices and Herbs
- Fresh basil
- Fresh chives
- Fresh cilantro
- Fresh mint
- Fresh oregano
- Fresh parsley
- Fresh rosemary
- Fresh thyme
- Cayenne pepper
- Chili powder
- Cinnamon
- Coarse sea salt
- Ground cumin
- Curry
- Garlic powder
- Garlic salt
- Grated Ginger
- Ground sage
- Herbes de provence
- Lemongrass
- Old Bay seasoning
- Onion powder
- Dried oregano

- Pepper
- Pumpkin pie spice (or a mix of nutmeg, cinnamon, all-spice, and ginger)
- Red pepper flakes
- Smoked paprika
- Sweet paprika
- Dried Thyme
- Turmeric

Frozen

- 1 cup frozen cherries
- 1 cup frozen raspberries
- ¼ cup frozen mixed berries

Vegetables & Fruit

- 2 tbsp 100% pineapple juice
- 12 oz fresh orange juice
- 1 small pineapple, sliced into 1/2 inch thick rings
- 2 large navel oranges
- 3 limes
- 10 lemons
- 2 oranges
- 2 bananas
- 20 garlic cloves
- 5 sweet potatoes
- 3 large russet potatoes
- 4 medium sweet onions
- 1 red onion, chopped
- 2 green onions, sliced
- 3 whole scallions, sliced into rings
- 1 shallot
- 10 cups baby spinach
- 4 cups kale
- 1 lb collard greens
- 1 lb cherry tomatoes
- 4 avocados
- 1 raw beet
- 1 red bell pepper
- 1 green bell pepper
- 1 jalapeño

- 1 zucchini
- 2 medium-large summer squash
- 1 butternut squash
- Persian cucumber
- 2 carrots
- 1 turnip, cut into 2" pieces
- 1 celery root, cut into 2" pieces
- 1 medium bulb fennel
- 1 oz shitake mushrooms, sliced
- 12 oz white mushrooms, halved
- 1 bunch of asparagus

Week 2 (and again on week 4)

A few of the ingredients on this list will come in larger containers and will keep throughout the entire month. Be sure to check your pantry before heading to the grocery store. These lists are created for a weekly shopping trip and not to stock up. Adjust as necessary.

Proteins
- 21 eggs
- 1 lb bacon
- 1 lb flank steak
- 2 lb pork roast
- 2 lb of ground pork
- 1 lb ground chicken
- 3 lb grass-fed ground beef
- 1 cup diced ham
- 2 whole chicken leg quarters
- 3 lb boneless skinless chicken thighs
- 1 lb chicken strips
- 1 lb chicken wings
- 2 lb salmon

Fats
- Avocado oil
- ¾ cup coconut oil
- ½ cup ghee

Nuts, Dried Fruit, & Seeds
- ¼ cup shredded coconut
- Roasted pumpkin seeds

Pantry
- ½ cup almond flour
- 1 tbsp coconut flour
- 1 ½ tsp baking powder
- 1 tbsp balsamic vinegar
- 1 ½ tsp apple cider vinegar
- 19.5 oz coconut milk
- 9 tbsp coconut aminos
- ¼ tsp fish sauce
- 2 ½ cups vegetable stock
- ½ cup chicken broth
- 3 tbsp pineapple juice
- ½ can artichoke hearts, quartered
- 1 tbsp capers
- 15 oz diced fire roasted tomatoes
- 2 (28 oz) cans crushed tomatoes
- ¼ cup Whole30 compliant hot sauce
- 1/4 cup date paste
- 2 tbsp brown mustard
- 2 cups pumpkin purée
- 2 tbsp chipotle in adobo sauce
- Skewers

Spices & Herbs
- Cayenne pepper
- Chili powder
- Cumin, ground
- Curry powder
- Fresh basil
- Fresh cilantro
- Fresh Italian parsley
- Garlic powder
- Italian seasoning
- Onion powder
- Paprika

- Parsley, dried
- Red pepper flakes
- Thai curry paste
- Thyme, dried
- Turmeric, ground
- Salt and pepper

Frozen
- 1 cup frozen strawberries

Vegetables & Fruit
- 1/3 cup blueberries
- 1 banana
- Fresh berries
- 2 lemons
- Chives
- 12 garlic cloves
- Ginger root
- 6 carrots
- 1 jicama
- 1 bunch of celery hearts
- 5 sweet potatoes
- 2 russet potatoes
- 8 red potatoes
- 5 white onions
- 2 purple onions
- 1 bunch green onions
- Scallions
- 2 red bell peppers
- 1 green bell pepper
- 2 jalapeños
- 8 oz mushrooms
- 4 cups spinach
- 2 cups chopped kale
- 1 head of cauliflower
- 1 head of green cabbage
- 2 zucchinis
- 1 butternut squash
- 16 oz broccoli cole slaw salad mix

- 2 avocados
- 4 roma tomatoes
- 4 medium broccoli crown, cut into florets about 1 ½ cups florets
- ¾ to 1 lb baby turnips
- 2 cups diced fresh broccoli

Holiday Meal Grocery List

Be sure to check your pantry before heading to the grocery store. This list is created for one holiday meal for 10 people. Throw in a vegetable tray or a bowl of nuts for appetizers. Lay out a few of your guests favorite, non compliant apps. This menu does not skimp on taste. Adjust as necessary.

Proteins
- Turducken (or turkey to keep it simple)
- 10 eggs

Fats
- ¾ cup duck fat
- 1 cup real butter

Nuts, Dried Fruit, & Seeds
- 1 cup pecans, chopped
- 2 ½ cups walnuts, finely chopped
- 1 cup raisins
- 7 cups cranberries
- 10 medjool dates

Pantry
- ¼ cup full-fat coconut milk
- 4 tbsp vanilla extract
- 8 cups almond flour
- 1/3 cup coconut flour
- 1 ½ cup arrowroot powder
- 3 tsp baking powder
- ½ tsp pumpkin pie spice
- 8 cups apple cider
- ¾ cup canned pumpkin

Spices & Herbs
- 5 tbsp fresh thyme
- 3 tbsp sage
- 1 tsp rosemary
- Salt & pepper
- 1 tsp whole cloves
- 1 tsp dried orange peel
- 2 cinnamon sticks
- 2 tbsp cinnamon
- 2 tbsp nutmeg

Vegetables & Fruits
- 2 lb Brussels sprouts
- 15 large sweet potatoes
- 4 cloves garlic
- 5 medium onions
- 1 bunch celery
- 8 crisp apples
- 5 apples
- 2 pears
- 1 lemon

Chapter 7: 30 Day Meal Plan

Week 1 & 3

In the recipe section you will find that the breakfast and lunch recipes are for 2 while the dinner recipes serve 4. This is for the ease of those who cook for more then just themselves come dinner time, whether it's for children or friends who join them. If you're eating alone simply divide it in half or use the extra portion for an upcoming meal. You will also find that recipes that call for coconut oil can be exchanged for extra virgin olive oil, animal fat, or clarified butter. Discover your preference and adjust the recipes accordingly.

Monday:
B - Kale & Sweet Potato Hash
L - Chicken & Zucchini Poppers
D - Chipotle Lime Chicken & Spinach Salad

Tuesday:
B - Avocado & Egg
L - Grilled Chicken & Tropical Fruit Salad
D - Roasted Turkey with Roasted Root Veggies

Wednesday:
B - Beet Berry Bowl
L - Citrus Shrimp Salad
D - Mint Lamb Chops

Thursday:
B - Almond Butter, Banana Smoothie
L - Thai Coconut Chicken Soup
D - Balsamic Flank Steak with Chimichurri Sauce

Friday:
B - Breakfast Veggie Bowl
L - Roasted Citrus Chicken Legs
D - Lemon Tilapia with Asparagus

Saturday:
B - Loaded Breakfast Potatoes
L - Artichoke & Tomato Salad
D - Citrus Shrimp & Steak

Sunday:
B - Pumpkin Pudding
L - Chicken & Summer Squash Sauté
D - Spicy Pork Tenderloin & Collard Greens

Week 2 & 4

Monday:
B - Zucchini Cakes with Fried Egg
L - Garlic Ginger Chicken
D - Sautéed Cabbage & Potatoes

Tuesday:
B - Veggie Bacon Egg Scramble
L - Curry Coconut Cauliflower Soup
D - Salmon & Prosciutto Roasted Asparagus

Wednesday:
B - Breakfast Salad
L - Bacon Wrapped, Coconut Chicken Nuggets
D - Chicken & Roasted Veggies

Thursday:
B - Breakfast Casserole
L - Artichoke Chicken Thighs
D - Pumpkin Chili

Friday:
B - Strawberry Kale Smoothie
L - Meatballs
D - Loaded Baked Potatoes (with leftover Pumpkin Chili)

Saturday:
B - Pork and Broccoli Slaw Frittata
L - Tomato Basil Beef Soup
D - Spicy Beef and Broccoli

Sunday:
B - Spinach Tomato Omelet
L - Buffalo Wings with Veggies
D - Pulled Pork Shoulder with Turnips

Tips:
- Add leftovers from dinner to breakfast, or save for lunch the next day.
- Keep a variety of raw vegetables, berries, and nuts on hand for mid day hunger. Treat yourself to apple slices and almond butter. Don't let yourself get over hungry. Make sure items that fit the Whole 30 are easily accessible.
- While this meal plan is set up for 3 meals a day remember that this is an individualized challenge. If your habits are to eat twice a day or five times a day adjust accordingly.
- If there is a recipe you do not like the first time do not remake it on the repeat week. Instead substitute it with one of your favorites from the list.
- For meal prepping lunches, if you do not have a lot of time to meal prep for lunches at work grill up a large batch of jalapeno or garlic ginger chicken. Freeze and defrost the night before. Add to left over veggies from previous dinner or add a quick side salad drizzled with Extra-virgin olive oil.

Chapter 8: Snacks

The key to success is simplicity. You can find delicious elaborate Whole30 snack recipes online. But, if you have to spend the entire day in the kitchen creating snacks and meals then you aren't breaking the obsession with food. Instead, food is still mastering you. Part of Whole30 is to break your addiction, not by moderation, but by elimination. One of the best ways to do this is to not dwell on what you can and cannot eat. Don't spend massive amounts of time in the kitchen where temptation lives. Below are some simple snack ideas to have on hand when hunger, hanger, and temptation strike.

Your head and determination should be making the calls, not your gut. Keep your head in the game and your stomach out of it!

- *Boiled eggs.* Keep a bowl of boiled, peeled eggs in the fridge. Make them a little fancier by keeping a batch of deviled eggs on hand. Mash up the yolks with hot sauce and Whole30 compliant mayonnaise. For a fun variation slice the boiled eggs, slather on the guacamole, and wrap in a slice of turkey. Two or three of those will make for an entire meal.

- *Sliced fruit*. Whether it's peaches, apples or pears sliced fruit is a light refreshing snack. Just like the boiled eggs it is simple to dress them up. Wrap in your favorite sliced meat and enjoy for a quick snack or make a meal out of it.

- *Mango avocado salsa*. This one is simple to make. One mango diced, one avocado diced, some chopped cilantro, and a squeeze of fresh lime juice. Eat with a spoon or with plantain chips.

- *Alternative chips*. The stores are full of alternative chips these days. Grab some kale chips, crispy green bean chips, or plantains.

- *Dried fruits and nuts*. Go easy on these, a few will get you far as they have a large amount of natural sugar. A handful of almonds is high in healthy fats and of all the nuts has the highest amount of fiber. These will keep you fuller longer.

- *Avocados*. Sprinkle with salt and eat straight from the peel. It is a filling satisfying snack full of healthy fats to keep you full.

- *Broth based Whole30 compliant soups* make for a great treat between meals. The combination of water, fibrous vegetables and the heat will leave you full and satisfied. So grab a mug full of your favorites on a cold morning and cuddle up on the couch for a few moments of quite. A cup of straight broth or one of many soups found online will do. For simplicity I make chicken noodle soup and leave out the noodles. If you have a Zoodler you can add zucchini in place of the noodles but I've found not having noodles is just as satisfying. Make an extra batch of the Thai-Style Coconut Chicken Soup found in Week 1 & 3, the Curry Coconut Cauliflower Soup or the Tomato Basil Beef Soup found in Week 2 & 4. Freeze it in individual paper cups, peel back the paper and place the cube in a microwave safe mug to reheat in the microwave. It's delicious and ready to go. Just double it up when you make it for lunch to save time in the kitchen.

- *Jerky*. This is an easy treat to hide in a purse or a car glove box. If you are feeling ambitious invest in a dehydrator. You'll save money and insure there are no added ingredients in your homemade jerky. You can also use it to make vegetable chips and to dehydrate your favorite fruits.

- *Canned protein*. Having canned chicken, salmon, and tuna come in handy for mid day hunger. Protein is great filler and mixed with some whole30 compliant mayo and cayenne pepper make for a tasty treat (plus cayenne pepper works as an appetite suppressant).

- *Smoked Salmon and Prosciutto*. These are delicious treats to have on hand and taste amazing wrapped around an apple slice or boiled egg.

If you work outside of the home, chances are you will be tempted by a snack, a donut, or that office boardroom lunch at some point in the 30 days. There are a number of Whole30 approved products outside of a can of nuts and dried fruit that you can keep on hand for such an emergency. Store a few in your glove box, in your purse, and in your office desk. Always be prepared. Here are just a few: Larabars, Seasnax Seawee Snax, Justin's Nut Butter Cups, Brooklyn Biltong, Oloves, Go Raw, Dang Coconut Chips, and Bare Organic Apple Chips.

If you are struggling with hunger on a regular basis during this journey don't shy away from the snacks or eating an extra meal. Whole30 is not about keeping track of calories or fat intake. It is about eliminating potentially problematic foods for your body. If you are always hungry you are always thinking about what you miss rather then feeling satisfied and empowered by this journey. Keep snacks accessible, meal prep, decide before going out to eat with family what you will order, and drink LOTS of water. This is your journey to health and wellness. With the proper preparation and mindset you will achieve your goal.

Chapter 9: RECIPES

Breakfast (Week 1 & 3)

Kale & Sweet Potato Hash

"It is with great sadness and a heavy heart that have to announce that I ate kale and liked it" – Greg Behrendt

The combination of kale, sweet potato, and spices feel like autumn in a bowl. They are divine and delicious nutritious dense way to begin a day. My suggestion over the next few weeks is to find two or three favorite go-to-breakfast dishes to continue with long after the Whole30 challenge is complete. If you've been hesitant to try kale, this recipe is the perfect place to change your mind.

Serves: 2
Time: 30-35 minutes stove top

Ingredients:
- 3 tbsp butter, or cooking fat of choice
- 2 medium sweet potatoes, peeled and dice into small cubes
- 1 medium onion, finely diced
- 1 tbsp minced garlic
- ¼ tsp ground sage
- 2 cups kale, finely chopped
- ¼ tsp smoked paprika
- ¼ tsp rosemary
- 1 tsp coarse sea salt

Method:
1. Melt butter in a frying pan over medium heat.
2. Add the sweet potatoes, onions, garlic and sage to the pan.
3. Stir and mix well, coating the vegetables in melted butter. Cook over medium heat, stirring occasionally, for 15 minutes.
4. Add kale, smoked paprika, rosemary and sea salt to the pan.
5. Cook for another 15-20 minutes or until the edges of the sweet potatoes brown and crisp. Potatoes should be tender and cooked through.
6. Serve with a sunny side up egg. Enjoy!

Avocado & Egg

"And perfect happiness? Man, that's a... the pool is about 92 degrees. The Jacuzzi is about 102 and an avocado farm." – Jamie Foxx

Two slices of bacon on the side and a dash of hot sauce and you could live on this meal. It is full of healthy fats and proteins essential to your body. It leaves you feeling full and satisfied for hours. A great way to start the day.

Serves: 2
Time: 15 minutes in the oven

Ingredients:
- 2 avocados
- 4 eggs
- Salt, to taste
- Pepper, to taste

Topping options:
- Cherry tomatoes, quartered
- Basil, chopped
- Chives, chopped

Method:
1. Preheat oven to 400.
2. Slice avocados in half and discard the pits.
3. Place the avocado halves on a baking sheet and scoop out a small amount of the flesh to make a hole large enough for one egg.
4. Crack one egg into each hole, season with salt and pepper.
5. Top with toppings of choice. Bake 15 minutes or until all of the egg white is cooked through and no longer translucent.
6. Sprinkle with fresh herbs. Enjoy!

Beet Berry Bowl

"I have some weird habits. For instance, I love beets. Show me a salad bar and I will clean them out of their beets." – Chris Pratt Read

You will either love beets or hate them. There is really no in between. They have a rich earthy aroma and taste. For those who discover they love this nutritiously rich food thinly slice a few, sprinkle with salt, and crisp in the oven. They make an excellent chip.

Serves: 2
Time: 5 minutes

Ingredients:
- 1 – 1 ½ cup plant based milk (almond or coconut)
- 1 banana, best if frozen
- 1 cup frozen cherries
- 1 cup frozen raspberries
- 1 raw beet (washed + peeled)
- 1 tbsp coconut butter or ghee

Topping options:
- pomegranate seeds, berries, sliced banana, coconut flakes

Method:
1. Place all ingredients in blender. Blend.
2. Pour into a bowl.
3. Top with pomegranate seeds, fresh berries, sliced banana, coconut flakes, and whatever else you love. Enjoy!

Banana Almond Smoothie

"Always take a banana to a party." – Steven Moffat

You won't find a lot of smoothies in this guide. Using them in the Whole30 challenge is highly debated. While the sugars are natural from the fruit it is still a large dump of sugar with very little protein. An egg and an avocado will set you up better to tackle temptations throughout the day. But who doesn't love a good smoothie? So we put a favorite with a little protein in it to help satiate your hunger.

Serves: 2
Time: 5 minutes

Ingredients:
- 8.5 oz full fat coconut milk
- 1 frozen banana

- 2 tbsp nut butter
- 1/8 tsp cinnamon

Optional Adds:
- 2 big handfuls of spinach or kale
- 1 tbsp coconut flakes
- ¼ cup frozen berries

Method:
1. Add all of the ingredients to your blender in the order listed above, and blend on high until creamy.
2. Pour into a glass, sprinkle with cinnamon. Enjoy!

Freeze For Later Directions:
1. After blending, pour each serving into quart sized freezer bag. Lay flat to freeze.
2. When ready to enjoy simply thaw slightly and pour contents into glass to enjoy.

Whole30 Tip:
Have ready made snacks and meals that are easily accessible to eliminate the excuse to cheat. Smoothies are easy to pre-make. Making a number of these reduces the amount of clean up time and easy to take on the go.

Roasted Veggie Breakfast Bowl with Fried Egg

"When you wake up in the morning, 'Pooh,' said Piglet at last, 'what's the first thing you say to yourself?'
'What's for breakfast?' said Pooh. 'What do you say, Piglet?'
'I say, I wonder what's going to happen exciting today?' said Piglet.
Pooh nodded thoughtfully. 'It's the same thing,' he said." – A.A. Milne

Have you ever woken up and thought, "what I really want for breakfast today is a salad?" No? Well this lands somewhere between a breakfast salad and a sweet potato hash. The smoky heat of spices mix well with the potato, onion and avocado leaving you feeling full and satisfied. A runny fried egg is the perfect topping as the yolk breaks and coats the vegetables beneath.

Serves: 2
Time: 20 minutes

Ingredients:

- 1 large sweet potato, cubed
- 1 large russet potato, cubed
- 1 red bell pepper, chopped
- ½ red onion, chopped
- 1 tsp chili powder
- ½ tsp smoked paprika
- ½ tsp turmeric
- ¼ tsp garlic powder
- ¼ tsp salt
- ⅛ tsp pepper
- 4 eggs
- 1 avocado, sliced
- Fresh herbs

Method:
1. Preheat oven to 375°F.
2. Grease baking sheet with coconut oil cooking spray.
3. Add potatoes, bell pepper, and onion in a bowl. Sprinkle with seasonings and toss until evenly coated.
4. In a single layer spread seasoned potatoes and veggies on prepared baking sheet. Roast for 10 minutes. Stir veggies. Bake another 10 minutes or until cooked through and tender.
5. Cook eggs in skillet over medium heat, sunny side up or to preference, while potatoes and vegetables are roasting.
6. Once veggies are done, remove from oven and divide into two bowls. Top with egg and avocado slices, garnish with fresh herbs. Enjoy!

Prep For Later Directions:
Double or triple this recipe if it is one of your favorites. After completing step 4 allow the potatoes to come to room temperature. Divide them into individual servings and store them in the quart size bags or Tupperware. When your ready to serve pull it out of the fridge and empty contents into a hot skillet (greased with a Whole30 compliant fat). Heat in skillet. This adds a nice crunch to the outside of your potatoes as well.
Place in bowl and using the same skillet prepare eggs to your preference. Over easy eggs provides a rich texture as the yolk breaks and runs through the veggies.

Whole30 Tip:
If you find a recipe you like, make extra to eat for leftovers the next day. Remove the recipes that you dislike and eat more of what you love. Even in the midst of an elimination diet, food is meant to be enjoyed, not dreaded.

Loaded Breakfast Potatoes

"My idea of heaven is a great big baked potato and someone to share it with." – Oprah Winfrey

This recipe takes careful planning or it may end up as brunch, or even a missed breakfast and lunch. Bake the potatoes the night before. In fact prep all the way through item 7 the night before. Then when you wake up pull them out of the fridge and pop them in the oven as it comes to temperature. Make a pot of coffee while you wait. Once the oven comes to temperature pull out the now warm potatoes and continue with steps 8 through 11. They'll be done before you finish your second cup of black coffee!

Serves: 2
Time: 1 hour 15 minutes

Ingredients:
- 2 medium sweet potatoes
- 4 slices bacon
- 1 medium sweet onion, diced
- 4 garlic cloves, minced
- Sea salt and black pepper
- 4 small eggs
- Fresh rosemary

Method:
1. Heat oven to 400°F.
2. Wrap sweet potatoes in foil and poke with a fork a couple times. Place directly on the oven rack. Cook for 40-45 minutes until soft. Remove and cool.
3. In a large skillet, fry bacon until crisp. Remove bacon and sauté the onion and garlic in bacon grease until the onion is translucent.
4. After bacon cools, dice into small pieces.
5. Cut baked sweet potatoes lengthwise then scoop out the middle of the sweet potato. Be careful not to break the skin.
6. Mash sweet potato into skillet. Cover and cook for 10 more minutes.
7. Stir in salt, pepper and half the bacon bits. Place sweet potatoes on a parchment lined baking sheet.
8. Scoop mash into potato shells. Create a large divot for the egg.
9. Break one egg into each divot and sprinkle with remaining bacon bits.

10. Cook for 15 minutes or until yoke is set and egg whites are cooked through.
11. Sprinkle with fresh chopped rosemary or a fresh herb of your choice. Enjoy!

Whole30 Tip:
Do the majority of this recipe the night before. Don't wait till you are already hungry to begin. You'll find yourself reaching for something nearby to satisfy you instead. The night before, while sitting down to dinner, have the potatoes baking in the oven. Then after dinner prepare through step 7. Cover the potatoes loosely and place in the fridge. The next morning pull them out, heat the oven to 400 degrees, and break one egg into each potato. Finish steps 8 to 9 and you will have a breakfast that could have taken half your morning in under 20 minutes.

Pumpkin Pudding

"Instead of doing cinnamon, nutmeg, and all those baking spices I'll have one spice that's for sweets, and that's pumpkin pie spice." – Sandra Lee

There is nothing better in the fall then pumpkin everything. Sandra Lee's advice is essential. In fact, if your missing the cream and sugar in your coffee (some find it the most difficult aspect of this diet) try sprinkling a little pumpkin pie spice into your cup. It will compliment this delicious breakfast pudding full of protein and vitamins. To cut back on the sweetness simply reduce or leave out the cranberries. Finely diced pecans also make an excellent garnish to this dish and add that extra punch of protein and healthy fats you need to feel fuller longer.

Serves: 2
Time: 20 minutes

Ingredients:
- 1/8 cup coconut sugar
- ¼ cup pumpkin puree
- ¼ cup coconut cream
- 1 ¼ cups coconut milk
- Pinch of salt
- 2 cups cooked cauliflower rice
- 1 tsp vanilla
- 1 tsp pumpkin pie spice (or a mix of nutmeg, cinnamon, all-spice, and ginger)
- 1/8 cup cranberries

Method:

1. Add coconut sugar, pumpkin puree, coconut cream, coconut milk, and salt to a large saucepan and bring to a simmer.
2. Add in the cooked cauliflower rice. Simmer, stirring frequently until the thick and creamy, about 10-15 minutes.
3. Remove from the heat. Add in the vanilla, pumpkin spice, and cranberries. Spoon into bowls and serve. Enjoy!

Whole30 Tip:
In addition to breakfast this makes for a great dessert or mid-day snack. Serve it warm or cold.

Lunch (Week 1 & 3)

Chicken & Zucchini Poppers

"Ask not what you can do for your country. Ask what's for lunch." – Orson Welles

This delicious dish is an easy one to make ahead of time and take to work. It heats up nicely in the microwave and has a delicious aroma of garlic and curry that will have your co-workers asking for a nibble. Make a few extra to share.

Serves: 2
Time: 10 minutes stovetop

Ingredients:
- ½ lb ground chicken breast
- 1 cup grated zucchini (leave peel on and squeeze out some of the liquid with paper towels or a clean kitchen towel)
- 2 green onions, sliced
- ½ bell pepper, diced
- 2 tbsp cilantro, minced
- 1 clove garlic
- ¼ tsp curry
- ½ tsp salt
- ½ tsp pepper
- 1 tbsp coconut oil, avocado oil, or ghee for cooking

Method:

1. Toss chicken with zucchini, green onion, bell pepper, cilantro, garlic, curry, salt, and pepper. Mixture will be very wet.
2. Make balls by scooping heaping tablespoons or using a cookie scoop.
3. Heat oil in a skillet over medium heat.
4. Cook balls for 10 minutes, 5 on each side or until golden brown and the centers are cooked through. Enjoy!

Grilled Pineapple Chicken

"Don't forget that fruit can be cooked - think of baked apples, poached pears and grilled pineapple. But if you like drinking fruit, blending will preserve more nutrition and fibre than juicing." – Michael Greger

Grilled pineapple transports me directly to the beach. The combination of coconut and tropical fruits pair nicely with the chicken. Grab a sparkling water and a slice of lime and find an hour to escape on a mental vacation.

Serves: 2
Time: 10 minutes

Ingredients:
- 1 tbsp coconut oil, melted
- 1 clove garlic, minced
- 1 tbsp date paste
- 1 tbsp coconut aminos
- 1 tsps picy brown mustard
- ½ tsp chili powder
- 2 tbsp 100% pineapple juice
- 1 lb boneless skinless chicken breasts, pounded to 1/2 inch thickness
- Salt
- ¼ tsponion powder
- ¼ tsp paprika
- 1small pineapple, sliced into 1/2 inch thick rings

Method:
1. Prepare the glaze by whisking together the first 7 ingredients. Divide in half and set aside. Keep at room temperature.
2. Sprinkle the chicken with sea salt, pepper, onion powder and smoked paprika on both sides. Brush with pineapple glaze.

3. Preheat your grill to medium high heat and generously brush with coconut oil. Add the chicken and brush with the glaze again. Cook on one side for 3-4 minutes before flipping. Brush on more glaze and continue to cook until just done, 3 more minutes. Depending on the thickness of your chicken you will need to adjust the time.
4. Grill the pineapple on med-high heat on an oiled grill until nicely caramelized. Sprinkle with sea salt.
5. Serve the chicken with the pineapple and remaining glaze/sauce set aside for serving.

Side Recommendation:
Serve with an assortment of tropical fruit and shredded coconut.

Whole30 Tip:
Some ingredients for the Whole30 may be difficult to come by. For instance date paste and coconut aminos may be new to you. Both of these ingredients are available on amazon if you cannot find them in your local grocery store.

*To make date paste, blend 1/3 cup dates (softened first in hot water if too dry) with 2 tbsp water in a high speed blender until pureed. Add drops of water as needed to create a smooth consistency.

Citrus Shrimp Salad with Fruit

"I make some of my best recipes with a simple homemade stock. Keep shrimp shells stored in a plastic bag in the freezer. When you have almost a gallon-bag full, you can make a stock in 30 minutes that you can use in soups and sauces. You can then freeze the stock in ice-cube trays." – Emeril Lagasse

Coconut is a stable of the Whole30 challenge and pairs nicely with both seafood and chicken. This shrimp salad is delicious. The only way to improve it is to make the dressing the nigh before to let it chill.

Serves: 2
Time: 15 minutes

Ingredients:
Dressing:
- 1 large navel orange
- 1 tsp coconut cream

- 1 tsp white wine vinegar
- Salt and freshly ground black pepper
- 2 tsp coconut oil

Salad:
- ¼ lb extra large shrimp, peeled and deveined, tails removed
- Pinch of Old Bay seasoning
- Salt
- 2 tsp coconut oil
- ½ medium ripe avocado, pitted and diced
- ½ Persian cucumber, thinly sliced into half moons
- ½ medium bulb fennel, trimmed, quartered, cored and very thinly sliced (on a mandoline or by hand), fronds reserved for garnish
- 4 cups baby spinach

Method:

Dressing:
1. Cut the top and bottom from an orange so it sits flat. Working top down, cut away the peel and pith to expose the flesh. Cut out the orange segments, leaving the membrane behind. Squeeze any juice from the membrane into a large bowl. You should have 1 Tbsp juice. Reserve the segments.
2. Whisk cream, vinegar, salt and several grinds of black pepper into the orange juice. While whisking, slowly pour in coconut oil. The dressing will be thick and creamy. Chill.

For the salad:
1. Sprinkle shrimp with Old Bay and salt.
2. Heat coconut oil in a large skillet over medium-high heat. Sear the shrimp until cooked through, about 3 minutes per batch. Remove to a plate to cool for 5 minutes.
3. Combine the shrimp, reserved orange segments, avocado, cucumber and fennel in the bowl with the dressing and toss gently until evenly coated.
4. Mound the spinach on two serving plates and top with the salad. Garnish with fennel fronds. Enjoy!

Thai-Style Coconut Chicken Soup

"Almost every culture has its own variation on chicken soup, and rightly so - it's one of the most gratifying dishes on the face of the Earth." – Yotam Ottolenghi

Soup is a comfort both on cold days and difficult ones. The heat from the ginger and cayenne pepper in this soup make it an excellent addition to a lunch thermos on a cold winter day. It's also a great way to love on a friend suffering from the sniffles. The creaminess from the coconut milk is soothing while being dairy free which is necessary for both Whole30 and an illness. There is something unique, a little bit of love in a bowl, that is found in chicken soup.

Serves: 2
Time: 1 hour

Ingredients:
- ½ quart chicken stock
- ½ lb chicken breasts, sliced into thin 2-inch strips
- 1 whole scallion, sliced into rings
- 1 stalk lemongrass, sliced into quarters (or 1 tbsp lemongrass paste)
- 2 tsp fresh grated ginger
- 2 tsp coconut aminos
- Splash of Whole30 compliant fish sauce
- ¼ tsp cayenne pepper (or more to taste)
- 1 oz shitake mushrooms, sliced
- 5 oz coconut milk
- 1/3 tsp fresh grated lime zest
- 1 tbsp fresh lime juice
- 2 tsp fresh chopped cilantro

Method:
1. Pour chicken stock in a large soup pot. Add the sliced chicken breast meat, sliced scallions, quartered lemon grass stalk, ginger, coconut aminos, fish sauce, and cayenne pepper.
2. Bring to a boil, then lower to medium heat to simmer. Simmer for 30 minutes.
3. After 30 minutes add the mushrooms and stir.
4. Turn the heat to low. Add coconut milk and stir.
5. Add lime zest and stir.
6. Slowly increase the heat, stirring constantly, till the soup reaches a slow simmer. Keep the soup at a slow simmer for 15 minutes, stirring often; do not let it boil.
7. After 15 minutes, remove from heat. Stir in the fresh lime juice and chopped cilantro.
8. Remove the lemon grass stalks with a slotted spoon.
9. Serve and enjoy!

Roasted Citrus And Herb Chicken Recipe

"I think the first thing you should learn is how to roast a chicken. Once you can roast a chicken, you can pretty much figure out anything else. And who doesn't like roasted chicken? It's a classic." – Haylie Duff

Learning how to roast a chicken is an essential tool for any chef. This recipe is light and fresh. It's an easy go to for future meal preps, easy meals, and a great way to impress the family. You can roast a full chicken or get pre-cut bone-in chicken parts for this simple recipe.

Serves: 2
Time: 1 hour

Ingredients:
- 1 ½ lb bone-in chicken parts
- 1 orange, sliced
- ½ lemon, sliced
- ½ onion, diced
- ½ cup fresh orange juice
- ½ cup fresh lemon juice
- 1 tbsp coconut oil
- 2 cloves garlic, minced
- 1 tsp dried oregano
- ¼ tsp paprika
- Pinch of red pepper flakes
- 2 fresh thyme sprigs
- 2 fresh rosemary sprigs
- Sea salt and freshly ground black pepper

Method:
1. Preheat your oven to 400°F.
2. In a bowl, combine coconut oil, garlic, orange juice, lemon juice, dried oregano, paprika, diced onion, red pepper flakes, and season with salt and pepper to taste.
3. Place half the orange slices and half the lemon slices at the bottom of a baking dish.
4. Arrange the chicken on top of the sliced citrus. Season to taste.
5. Top the chicken with the fresh herbs and remaining citrus slices.
6. Drizzle the orange-lemon juice mixture (from step 2) over the chicken.

7. Place in the preheated oven and bake, uncovered, for 45 to 60 minutes.
8. Enjoy!

Artichoke & Tomato Salad

"My love for artichokes comes from when I was very young. My mother and father would slice the hearts and fry them, and they would be crispy around the leaves and tender at the base." – Jose Andres

This recipe calls for artichoke hearts from a jar, which for ease I recommend. However if you have a little extra time on your hand learning to roast your own artichokes is a great skill to have. They make for wonderful appetizers huddled around Monday night football games or sitting around the table with friends. A quick dip made from Whole30 compliant mayo and chipotle, or a simple melted clarified butter, are the perfect-dipping companions to this delicious treat.

Serves: 2
Time: 5 minutes, no cook

Ingredients
- ½ lb cherry tomatoes, sliced in half
- Salt and pepper to taste
- ¼ jar (7 ½ oz) marinated quartered artichoke hearts, drained
- 1 tsp minced fresh parsley
- 1 tsp lemon juice
- 1 garlic cloves, minced
- 1 tbsp fresh thyme

Method:
1. Slice the tomatoes and place on a large plate.
2. Sprinkle with salt and pepper.
3. In a small bowl, toss remaining ingredients.
4. Spoon over tomatoes. Enjoy! .

Whole30 Tip:
Play around with these recipes and add favorite Whole30 compliant ingredients. Change out the lemon juice for vinegar and add walnuts or a handful of black olives. Switch out the thyme for basil. Have fun creating new dishes. For a good idea of what foods pair well together grab a copy of <u>The Flavor Bible</u> by Karen Page and Andrew Dornenburg.

Chicken and Summer Squash Sauté

"You know, when you get your first asparagus, or your first acorn squash, or your first really good tomato of the season, those are the moments that define the cook's year. I get more excited by that than anything else." – Mario Batali

Depending on the time of year you may or may not have summer squash readily available. Throughout this guide substitute various ingredients for fresh seasonal ones. Zucchini may be more available, if so use it. The freshest ingredients are the ones you want to use for optimal taste and nutrition.

Serves: 2
Time: 25 minutes

Ingredients:
- 3 tbsp coconut oil, divided
- ½ lb chicken breasts, chopped into large chunks
- 2 medium-large summer squash, thinly sliced
- 1 medium onion, halved and thinly sliced
- 3 cloves garlic, minced
- Sea salt and ground pepper to taste
- Fresh lemon wedges, for serving
- Fresh rosemary for garnish

Method:
1. Heat the oil in a large skillet (or wok) over medium-high heat. Season the chicken on both sides with salt and pepper. Add the chicken to the hot oil and let it sear, 4-5 minutes on each side. Transfer the chicken to a bowl and set aside.
2. Add the squash and onion to the hot pan. Season with salt and pepepr. Stir occasionally until the vegetables are tender and start to brown, about 6 to 8 minutes.
3. Add the garlic and saute 1 minute more.
4. Add the chicken and cook for 1 minute.
5. Squeeze fresh lemon juice and sprinkle fresh rosemary over the dish.
6. Serve and enjoy!

Dinner (Week 1 & 3)

Chiptole Lime Chicken

"Chipotles to me are a one-of-a-kind pepper because they're smoked jalapenos, so they're fiery and they're smoky. It's good to use chipotles in salsas or soups or condiments - that works really well. To me, they always really pick up anything you put them in." – Bobby Flay

A little heat in the kitchen is a good thing. Play around with your favorites. Add additional chipotle or jalapeno to this dish to kick it up a notch. If spicy isn't to your liking then reduce the amount of chipotle to 1 1/2 tsp. The more you enjoy your food the better success you will find. Play around with the recipes to your liking.

Serves: 4
Time: 20 minutes

Ingredients:
- 2 lb of chicken breasts
- 2 limes
- 1 tbsp chiptole (to taste, or 1 jalapeno)
- 4 tbsp coconut oil
- 2 tbsp coconut amino
- 1 tbsp garlic powder
- 1 tsp red pepper flakes
- 1 small handful of cilantro
- Salt and pepper to taste

Method:
1. Zest both limes and add to a medium mixing bowl.
2. Juice both limes, and add the juice to the bowl.
3. Add the chipotle to the lime juice. (If using a fresh jalapeno remove the seeds and membrane to reduce the heat.)
4. Add the remaining ingredients to the bowl.
5. Use a high-powered blender until smooth.
6. Put the chicken in a bowl or gallon Ziploc bag. Pour the marinade over the chicken.
7. Refrigerate and let sit for a minimum of 3 hours, can be prepared for up to 24 hours ahead.
8. Grill or bake the chicken until it reaches an internal temperature of 180 degrees.

Freeze For Later Directions:
1. Do steps 1-6. On step six use a galloon freezer bag. Lay flat to freeze.

2. When ready to enjoy simply thaw in refrigerator overnight then resume with step 8 once dinner time approaches. This can be kept frozen for a month.

Spinach Side Salad:
While the chicken is cooking toss together a salad to serve with it. In a big bowl combine spinach, basil, chard, chives, maybe some leftover bacon crumbles or your favorite nuts. Just toss in what you love, sprinkle a little salt and squeeze fresh lime juice over the salad in place of dressing. It's the perfect side to accompany the chiptole lime chicken.

Roast Turkey with Root Vegetables

"What a marvelous resource soup is for the thrifty cook - it solves the ham-bone and lamb-bone problems, the everlasting Thanksgiving turkey, the extra vegetables." – Julia Child

Make your kitchen smell like Thanksgiving. In fact tuck this one away for this year's feast. It's the main course and a side all in one, and best of all its Whole30 compliant. Skip forward to the Holiday Guide section to discover some great sides to go with this roast turkey.

Serves: 4
Time: 1 hour 30 minutes

Ingredients:
- 6 tbsp ghee or clarified butter
- 2 tbsp minced flat-leaf parsley
- 1 ½ tsp ground cumin
- 1 ½ tsp sweet paprika
- 1 shallot, minced
- 1 (6 lb.) turkey, cut into 4 pieces
- Kosher salt and freshly ground black pepper, to taste
- 2 medium potatoes, cut into 2" pieces
- 2 carrots, cut into 2" pieces
- 1 turnip, cut into 2" pieces
- 1 celery root, cut into 2" pieces
- ½ butternut squash, peeled, seeded, and cut into 2" pieces
- 1 tbsp extra-virgin olive oil
- 2 sprigs each fresh thyme and rosemary

Method:
1. Heat oven to 500°F.
2. In a bowl, mix butter, parsley, cumin, paprika, and shallots; set aside.
3. Season turkey with salt and pepper.
4. Loosen turkey skin; rub ghee under skin.
5. Combine root vegetables and squash in a bowl. Drizzle with oil, season with salt and pepper, and toss.
6. Transfer vegetables to a large roasting pan. Spread to cover bottom. Arrange thyme and rosemary over vegetables. Arrange turkey over herbs and vegetables.
7. Roast turkey for 20 minutes. Reduce heat to 350°F; roast until an instant-read thermometer inserted into each turkey breast reads 150° and each leg, thigh, and wing reads 160°, about 1 hour. (Some pieces will be done before others.)
8. Continue cooking vegetables until tender. Discard herbs; transfer vegetables to a serving platter along with turkey and tent with foil to keep warm.

Whole30 Tip:
When enjoying a meal like this one with those who are not on the Whole30 diet, like children, simply add additional side dishes to fill them up. Rolls and gravy made from the drippings would complement this dish well. If these items are tempting to you put them at the other end of the table out of your reach. Fresh fruit sprinkled with coconut flakes is also a great side to go with any meal and is compliant.

Holiday Guide:
Triple up this recipe to serve a crowd at Thanksgiving. Find some delicious sides to accompany this dish in the holiday guide found later in this book. If you are in the midst of the holiday season when starting this challenge offer to host or bring dishes to the feast in order to make sure there are at least a few Whole30 compliant dishes you can endulge in.

Mint Lamb Chops

"It's long been a cliché in Washington that if you hang a lamb chop in your window, guests will come." – Suzanne Fields

If roast turkey takes you to Thanksgiving these Mint Lamb Chops with Hasselback Potatoes will take you straight to Christmas.

Serves: 4
Time: 20 minutes

Ingredients:
- 4 lamb chops
- 1/3 cup coconut oil
- 2 garlic cloves, minced
- 2 tsp fresh oregano, minced
- 2 tsp fresh lemon zest
- 1 tbsp whole-grain mustard
- 1 tbsp. white wine vinegar
- 2 tbsp mint leaves, minced
- Sea salt and freshly ground black pepper

Method:
1. Preheat a grill to medium-high.
2. Season the lamb chops to taste with sea salt and black pepper.
3. In a bowl, combine oil, garlic, oregano, and lemon zest.
4. Brush the chops generously with the oregano-garlic oil.
5. Cook the lamb chops for 4 to 5 minutes per side on the preheated grill.
6. Let the lamb chops rest for 5 minutes.
7. In a bowl, whisk together the mustard, white wine vinegar, mint, and season with salt and pepper to taste.
8. Serve the lamb chops with the mint sauce drizzled on top.

Hasselback Potatoes

Hasselback Potatoes make a great side for this dish. You'll want to get these started before the lamb chops though as they take significantly longer to cook. These potatoes will take 60 to 70 minutes.

Ingredients:
- 4 large potatoes, Yukon Gold, Russet, or Red Bliss
- 4 tbsp coconut oil
- Salt and Pepper to taste
- Fresh oregano and mint, minced

Method:
1. Heat the oven to 425°F with a rack in the lower-middle position.
2. Scrub the potatoes clean and pat them dry.

3. Cut slits in the potatoes, leaving the bottom intact: Cut slits into the potato, stopping just before you cut through so that the slices stay connected at the bottom of the potato. Space the slices 1/4-inch apart.
4. Brush the potatoes with half the oil. Arrange the potatoes in a baking dish.
5. Sprinkle with salt and pepper.
6. Bake 30 minutes, then brush with oil. Nudge the layers slightly apart if sticking together and make sure the oil drips into the slits.
7. Bake for another 30 to 40 minutes, until the potatoes are crispy on the edges and easily pierced in the middles with a paring knife. Stuff the oregano and mint into the slits and sprinkle over the top 5 to 10 minutes before the end of cooking.
8. Serve immediately and enjoy!

Holiday Tip:
Add this recipe to your Christmas or Easter menu. No one but you will know you are eliminating foods. No one has asked you to eliminate taste. Over time you will find that the Whole30 compliant meals offer a richer flavor with nutrient dense ingredients.

Balsamic Flank Steak with Mushrooms

"The secret of food lies in memory - of thinking and then knowing what the taste of cinnamon or steak is." – Jerry Saltz

The best part of Whole30 is that we aren't skimping on taste. Done correctly you won't notice what you are missing because you'll be to busy enjoying what you are eating as well as how you are beginning to feel. For those in the family not on the Whole30 Meal Plan with you throw a bowl of instant mashed potatoes on the table. Fill them up so there's more of the good stuff for you!

Serves: 4
Time: 10 minutes (Marinade overnight)

Ingredients
Steak:
- 3 lb flank steak (preferably grass-fed)
- 1 cup balsamic vinaigrette
- 2 tsp black pepper

Chimichurri Sauce:
- 2 cup fresh parsley
- 2 large clove garlic

- 1/3 cup avocado oil
- ½ tsp salt
- ¼ tsp black pepper
- Juice of 1 lemon
- Pinch of red pepper flakes

Method:
1. Place flank steaks in a large zip-top bag. Add vinaigrette. Seal bag and gently massage steak to coat. Place in refrigerator to marinate up to 24 hours.
2. When ready to prepare steaks, remove bag from the fridge and allow it to sit at room temperature for 20 minutes while grill preheats.
3. Preheat grill to high heat (400-450°F)
4. Remove steaks from bag and place on a clean plate. Sprinkle both sides with black pepper.
5. When grill is hot, remove steak from bag and discard marinade. Place on grill grate over direct heat. Grill 5-6 minutes then flip steak and grill an additional 5-6 minutes or until desired cook is attained. Note: Flank steak is best served medium-rare.
6. Remove steaks to a clean plate and allow to rest for 5 minutes before slicing diagonally across the grain.

Balsamic Mushrooms

Ingredients
- ¼ cup olive oil
- 12 oz white mushrooms, halved (quartered if large)
- 3 tbsp balsamic vinegar
- Salt and pepper to taste
- ¼ tsp red pepper flakes

Instructions
1. Heat oil in a skillet over medium-high heat.
2. Add mushrooms, and cook until golden brown, about 5 minutes.
3. Stir in vinegar, salt, and red pepper flakes, and season with pepper.
4. Cook 1 more minute. Transfer to a bowl, and serve.

Lemon Tilapia with Asparagus

"Someone may offer you a freshly caught whole large fish, like a salmon or striped bass. Don't panic – take it!" – Julia Child

My philosophy is whenever fresh fish is put in front of me I eat it. There is nothing better then the flakiness of tilapia and the acidity of lemons. If you discover your missing a few of these ingredients a simple squeeze of lemon juice, a douse in melted clarified butter, with a little garlic and salt will still deliver a delicious Whole30 compliant meal. You can't go wrong with Tilapia and lemon.

Serves: 4
Time: 25 minutes

Ingredients:
Lemon Tilapia:
- 4 tilapia fillets
- 6 tbsp lemon juice
- 1 ½ tsp sea salt flakes
- ¼ tsp ground black pepper
- ¼ tsp thyme
- ¼ tsp herbes de provence
- ¼ tsp garlic salt
- 2 tbsp pine nuts
- ¼ tsp lemon zest
- A few thinly sliced lemon slices

Lemon Asparagus:
- 1 tbsp coconut oil
- 2 tbsp lemon juice
- 1 bunch of asparagus
- Salt and Pepper to taste

Method:
1. Preheat the oven to 375°F.
2. Place the tilapia fillets into a large pan. Add lemon juice.
3. In a small bowl, mix the sea salt flakes, ground black pepper, thyme, herbs de provence, and garlic salt. Sprinkle the seasoning on top of the tilapia.
4. Add the pine nuts to the pan.
5. Top the fillets with the lemon slices and sprinkle the lemon zest onto them. Set the pan aside.
6. Next, cover a cookie sheet in foil.
7. Cut the bottom hard parts of the asparagus off (about 1-2 inches) and lay the asparagus evenly across the cookie sheet.

8. Evenly pour 1 tbsp of oil over the asparagus. Evenly pour 2 tbsp of lemon juice on top of the asparagus.
9. Salt and pepper to taste.
10. Place the cookie sheet full of the asparagus onto the lower rack of the oven. Put the pan with the tilapia on the top rack of the oven.
11. Bake for 25 minutes. The tilapia is ready when it is white and flakes with a fork.
12. Serve and enjoy!

Citrus Shrimp & Steak

"My favorite thing is to have a big dinner with friends and talk about life." – Carla Gugino

It's a citrus surf 'n' turf Whole30 style. Remember to save your shrimp peels to freeze for stock. It will make an excellent broth to sip on for snacking during cooler days.

Serves: 4
Time: 15 minutes

Ingredients:
- 1 tbsp ghee
- 1 cup fresh orange juice
- ½ cup fresh lemon juice
- 4 garlic cloves, minced
- 2 tbsp finely chopped onion
- 1 tbsp chopped fresh parsley
- ½ tsp freshly ground black pepper
- 3 lb medium shrimp, peeled and deveined
- 2 lb steak, cut into chunks
- 1 medium orange, cut into wedges
- 1 medium lemon, cut into wedges

Method:
1. In a medium bowl, whisk together the oil, orange juice, lemon juice, ¾ of the garlic, 1 tbsp of the onion, 2 teaspoons of the parsley and pepper.
2. Pour the mixture into a large skillet set over medium heat. Bring to a simmer and cook until reduced by half, 5 to 8 minutes.
3. Add the shrimp, cover, and cook until the shrimp turns pink, about 5 minutes.

4. At the same time cook the steak in a hot skillet with 1 tbsp of onion and ¼ of the garlic.
5. After the steak is finished cooking add it to the same serving dish as the shrimp.
6. Top with the remaining parsley. Serve with the orange and lemon wedges on the side.

Whole30 Tip:

If you have extras from lunch the artichoke and tomato salad would be a great side with this dish. If not a quick side salad with lemon juice for the dressing would compliment it well. Don't avoid social dinners during this time. Try to keep as much normalcy as possible. Invite friends over for dinner and conversation. Have a movie night in where you can make snacks that you can participate (or simply smuggle in a can of nuts to your favorite movie theater).

Spicy Pork Tenderloin & Collard Greens

"My mom's collard greens. No one else in the world can make them like hers. I'm not just saying that because she's my mom. She's got some Mississippi secret. I could seriously eat them every day." – Santigold

If you're from the south you know a "mess of greens" is essential to any meal plan. This recipe will have your mouth watering and your family ready for dinner in no time.

Serves: 4
Time: 15 minutes

Ingredients:
- 1 tbsp chili powder
- 1 tsp dried thyme
- ¼ tsp cayenne pepper
- Kosher salt and freshly ground black pepper
- 2 small pork tenderloins (about 12 ounces each)
- 3 tablespoons coconut oil
- 1 bunch collard greens (about 1 pound), stems removed, leaves thinly sliced
- ½ cup jarred Peppadew peppers, drained and roughly chopped
- 2 scallions, thinly sliced
- 2 tbsp apple cider vinegar

Method:
1. Preheat the oven to 475°F.

2. Combine the chili powder, thyme, cayenne and 3/4 teaspoon each salt and black pepper in a small bowl.
3. Rub the pork with 1 tbsp oil and then the spice mixture.
4. Transfer to the prepared pan and roast, turning once, until a thermometer inserted into the center of the pork registers 145°F, about 15 minutes.
5. Transfer to a cutting board; let rest.
6. Meanwhile, combine the collard greens, 1 tbsp oil and ¼ tsp salt in a large bowl. Massage the greens with your hands until slightly wilted, about 1 minute. Add the Peppadews, scallions, vinegar and the remaining 1 tbsp oil; season with salt and black pepper and toss to combine. Set aside.
7. Slice the pork and serve with the collard greens. Enjoy!

Breakfast (Week 2 & 4)

Zucchini Cakes with Fried Egg

"Why, sometimes I've believed as many as six impossible things before breakfast." – Lewis Carroll, Alice in Wonderland

This recipe works just as well with grated zucchinis as it does with grated. There is no need to run out and get new kitchen gadgets when chances are you have everything you need already. A fried egg is the perfect topper to these zucchini cakes.

Serves: 2
Time: 15 minutes

Ingredients:
- 2 medium zucchinis, grated or zoodled
- 1 tsp salt (divided, 1/2 tsp. to release moisture and 1/2 tsp. to add to mixture)
- ¼ cup almond flour
- 1 egg, beaten
- 2 eggs, to fry
- 3 tbsp chives, finely chopped
- Salt & pepper
- Avocado oil, to coat pan

Method:
1. Grate the grated or zoodled zucchini in a colandar in the sink and toss with 1/2 tsp salt.

2. Let stand 10 minutes.
3. Then wring excess water out of zucchini with paper towels or clean kitchen towel.
4. Place all ingredients into large mixing bowl and gently mix it all together.
5. Coat bottom of skillet with oil of choice (we used avocado oil) and bring the temperature to medium high.
6. Drop 1/4 cup of mixture into your skillet, be delicate it will be a little fragile until cooked.
7. Flatten zucchini mixture and fry both sides till a golden color, approximately 5 minutes per side.
8. Place cooked zucchini fritters on paper towel to absorb any excess oil.
9. Salt & pepper fritters.
10. Fry an egg, sunny side up, and slide onto your fritter.
11. Enjoy!

Veggie Bacon Egg Scramble

"Breakfast is the most important meal of the day. When you feed yourself what your body needs when it needs it, that's love. So give your bod some TLC and sit down and enjoy a good, substantial breakfast." – Kathy Freston

Eggs make for a great breakfast however you prepare them. They are filling and full of protein keeping you full longer and out of the kitchen. Don't skimp on breakfast. Use it as a time to fuel up and prepare for the day ahead.

Serves: 2
Time: 5-10 minutes

Ingredients:
- 2 pieces of uncooked bacon, coarsely chopped
- ¼ small onion, coarsely chopped
- ¼ red bell pepper, seeds removed and coarsely chopped
- 3 brown mushrooms, coarsely chopped
- Handful of baby spinach
- 2 large eggs
- 1 small avocado

Method:
1. Place chopped bacon in a non-stick pan and heat over medium-high heat until bacon is cooked but not crisp.
2. Leave the bacon fat in the pan to cook with.

3. Add onions and bell peppers to the pan and cook until onions soften and are translucent.
4. Add mushrooms and stir.
5. Add spinach.
6. In a small bowl, scramble the eggs.
7. Stir veggies in skillet to wilt spinach and pour eggs over the vegetables.
8. Tilt pan so that the egg spreads across the entire pan.
9. Let cook for a moment and then stir the ingredients so the egg cooks throughout.
10. Continue cooking until eggs are cooked through.
11. Plate. Slice avocado and place on top of the eggs. Enjoy!

Breakfast Salad

"A well-made salad must have a certain uniformity; it should make perfect sense for those ingredients to share a bowl." – Yotam Ottolenghi

You've had breakfast for dinner but have you had dinner for breakfast? This breakfast salad is the perfect treat with sunny side up fried eggs and sliced avocado. It will fill you up and leave you satisfied.

Serves: 2
Time: 15 minutes

Ingredients:
- 1 1/3 cup butternut squash, peeled and chopped
- 1/3 cup red onion or shallot, chopped
- 1 ½ tbsp coconut oil or ghee
- 12 oz broccoli cole slaw salad mix
- 1 tbsp balsamic vinegar
- 1 tbsp water
- ¼ tsp minced garlic or one garlic clove minced
- ¼ tsp or more sea salt and black pepper each (to taste)
- 1/3 cup blueberries
- 4 eggs
- Red pepper flakes and cilantro to garnish
- 1 avocado, sliced
- Roasted pumpkin seeds (optional)

Method:

1. Place chopped squash in a microwave safe dish with 1 tbsp water. Steam for 2 - 2.5 minutes or more. Depends on microwave power. Cook until tender, not mushy.
2. Remove, drain, set aside.
3. In a small skillet, place 1 tbsp butter or oil.
4. Heat on medium high and add onions.
5. Fry for 2 minutes until the onions start to brown.
6. Next add in slaw, garlic, salt/pepper, 1 tbsp water, and balsamic vinegar.
7. Mix all together in skillet.
8. Cover and cook over medium heat for 2-3 minutes.
9. Slaw will be tender but not fully cooked.
10. Remove and place in bowl.
11. Add squash and 1/3 cup berries to the bowl, toss.
12. Fry your eggs in the same skillet.
13. Add another 1/2 tbsp of butter or oil over medium high heat.
14. Fry until crispy on outside and yolk is to your preference.
15. Spoon slaw onto plates.
16. Place fried egg on top of slaw.
17. Garnish with red pepper, 1 tbsp pumpkin seeds, cilantro, and any extra seasoning.
18. Serve with sliced avocado and enjoy!

Whole30 Tip:
Keep fresh berries, nuts, and avocados on hand. They make quick easy snacks and garnishes for many of the Whole30 recipes. Having easy to access snacks to keep cravings at bay will help you succeed with this lifestyle change.

Breakfast Casserole

"I am huge on bold, strong flavors, and I think every aspect of a dish should be thoughtful, whether it's the chicken on top of a Cobb salad or the topping on a savory casserole." – Chrissy Teigen

Every meal plan should have a breakfast casserole or two, Whole30 is no different. Filled with pork, sweet potatoes, mushrooms, and veggies this is a casserole you'll want to use again and again. While most egg casseroles are filled with dairy and hash browns this one is full of nutritiously dense ingredients that will power you for the day ahead.

Serves: 2

Time: 1 hour

Ingredients:
- 4 eggs
- 1/3 cup full-fat coconut milk
- ½ lb ground pork
- ¾ cups sweet potatoes, shredded
- ½ onion, diced
- 1 garlic clove, minced
- 3 button mushrooms, sliced
- ½ bell pepper, diced
- 1 green onion, sliced
- Cooking fat
- Sea salt and freshly ground black pepper

Method:
1. Preheat oven to 350°F.
2. Melt cooking fat in a skillet over medium heat.
3. Cook the onion and garlic 1 to 2 minutes until the onions are translucent.
4. Add in the sausages and break apart while cooking for 5 to 6 minutes.
5. Place the shredded potatoes at the bottom of a small casserole dish and top with the onion-sausage mixture.
6. Add the bell pepper and mushrooms to the casserole.
7. In a large bowl, whisk together eggs and coconut milk; season with salt and pepper to taste.
8. Pour in the eggs on top of the sausage mixture.
9. Cover and cook for 1 hour. Top with green onions and enjoy.

Tip:
This can be cooked in a slow cooker overnight for the whole family. Adjust the ingredients as follows; prepare using instructions 1-8, and cook on low for 6 to 8 hours in the slow cooker.
- 12 eggs
- 1 cup full-fat coconut milk
- 2 lb ground pork
- 2 cups sweet potatoes, shredded
- 1 onion, diced
- 2 garlic clove, minced
- 8 button mushrooms, sliced
- 1 bell pepper, diced

- 2 green onion, sliced
- Cooking fat
- Sea salt and freshly ground black pepper

Kale and Strawberry Smoothie

"Kale is my best friend. I eat kale salad. I put kale in my smoothies, kale in my soup. Kale, kale, kale! I feel like Popeye. I love it. I definitely need variety or I get super bored, so I have to mix it up with different sauces and tahini or whatever." – Alanis Morissette

While daily smoothies are discouraged, this is a delightfully refreshing smoothie that can be used throughout the day as a snack or in the morning for a quick meal before your morning commutes. The best part of adding smoothies to the Whole30 challenge is ease and convenience.

Serves: 2
Time: 5 minutes

Ingredients:
- 8 oz coconut milk
- 1 cup frozen strawberries
- 2 cups chopped kale
- ½ cup ice or ½ frozen banana

Method:
Put all ingredients in blender and mix until smooth. Serve and enjoy!

Freeze For Later Directions:
1. After blending, pour each serving into quart sized freezer bag. Lay flat to freeze.
2. When ready to enjoy simply thaw slightly and pour contents into glass to enjoy.

Pork and Broccoli Slaw Frittata

"Are you cooking a frittata in a sauce pan? What is this prison?" – Schmidt, <u>New Girl</u>

Have you ever made a frittata? They are not as difficult as they sound and are a great way to hide vegetables and ingredients picky eaters may not otherwise try. Hide them in this puffy delicious egg and suddenly they'll be devouring them. This broccoli slaw frittata is an excellent first. Overtime mix and match other Whole30 compliant ingredients to create the perfect frittata for you.

Serves: 2
Time: 30-35 minutes

Ingredients:
- 1 tbsp coconut oil
- ½ onion, thinly sliced
- Salt
- ½ lb of ground pork
- 1 clove garlic, minced
- 3 large eggs
- 2 tbsp coconut milk
- 1 tsp curry powder
- Freshly ground black pepper
- 2 tbsp roughly chopped Italian parsley
- ½ cup shredded broccoli slaw
- ¼ cup shredded carrots

Method:
1. Preheat the oven to 350°F.
2. Heat the coconut oil over medium heat in a small cast-iron skillet.
3. Sauté onions, season with salt, until translucent.
4. Add the pork and garlic, cook until no longer pink.
5. While the pork is cooking, whisk together the eggs, coconut milk, curry powder, salt, pepper, and parsley.
6. Once the pork is cooked add the broccoli slaw and carrots to the skillet. Season with salt and pepper.
7. Pour the egg mixture into the pan, cover and cook for 5 minutes to set the bottom.
8. Put into preheated oven and bake for 20 minutes.
9. Edges will be brown and puffy, and center will be firm when done.
10. Slice and enjoy!

Spinach Tomato Omelet

"If you look upon ham and eggs and lust, you have already committed breakfast in your heart." – C. S. Lewis

Omelets are simple. It's just a few whisked eggs and a few favorite ingredients added in. Then fold and flip and a slide onto the plate. Douse it in hot sauce or add sliced avocado for extra flavor.

Serves: 2
Time: 10 minutes

Ingredients:
- 4 eggs
- 2 cups spinach
- 2 diced tomatoes
- 1 cup diced ham
- ½ onion, diced

Method:
1. Whisk the eggs in a bowl.
2. Chop up some spinach and add half of it to the egg mix.
3. Chop tomatoes, onions and ham.
4. Add preferred oil to a hot skillet.
5. Put in the onions and sauté till translucent. Add ham and tomatoes until the ham is browned. Add remaining spinach to wilt.
6. Remove the onions, ham, tomato, and spinach from pan and set aside.
7. Add more oil to the pan and heat up.
8. Pour in mixed eggs with spinach and adjust heat to low. Cover the pan.
9. When the top looks almost done, flip the egg over.
10. Put the cooked onions, ham, tomato, and spinach from earlier over one half of the omelet.
11. Fold the omelet and serve.
12. Enjoy!

Lunch (Week 2 & 4)

Garlic Ginger Chicken

"Onions, along with leeks, garlic, shallots and scallions, make up the allium family of vegetables, which can have beneficial effects on the cardiovascular and immune systems, as well as possible anti-diabetic and anti-cancer effects." – Joel Fuhrman

Ginger is one of those ingredients you should always have on hand. It soothes indigestion problems and inflammation. It adds a spicy kick of heat to any dish.

Serves: 2
Time: 10 minutes
Pair with: stir-fried vegetables or cauliflower rice.

Ingredients:
- 2 whole chicken leg Quarters
- 1 tbsp ghee
- 3 cloves garlic, mashed and minced
- 2 tsp ginger root, minced
- 2 tbsp coconut aminos
- ¼ tsp fish sauce, Whole30 compliant
- Pepper and salt to taste

Method:
1. Preheat the oven to bake at 425°F.
2. In a small saucepan, melt ghee on low heat.
3. Raise heat to medium and add ginger, garlic, fish sauce, and coconut aminos to the ghee.
4. Allow mixture to come to a bubble, and allow to bubble while stirring for a minute or two, then remove from heat.
5. Place chicken legs in an oven save baking dish.
6. Pour sauce over each chicken leg.
7. Sprinkle each leg with salt and pepper.
8. Bake chicken at 425 for 45 minutes.
9. Allow chicken to cool for 30-45 minutes and then enjoy.

Curry Coconut Cauliflower Soup

"The first meal my husband ever made me was a chicken curry. I have never tasted anything so delicious in my life." – Lesley Nicol

This Curry Coconut Cauliflower Soup is delightful. Full of flavor from the ginger, turmeric, and curry. It will warm you up on the coldest day. You will want more then one bowl.

Serves: 2
Time: 40 minutes

Ingredients:
- ½ head of cauliflower, roughly chopped
- 1 ½ tsp coconut oil
- ½ tsp sea salt
- 1/2 medium onion, chopped
- 2 large carrots, chopped
- 1tbsp ginger, chopped
- 1 garlic cloves, crushed with your knife
- ½ tsp ground turmeric
- 2 tbsp Thai curry paste (see notes)
- 2 ½ cups vegetable stock
- ½ cup coconut milk
- Sea salt, to taste
- Sliced green onion, chili peppers, cilantro, chili oil and/or freshly squeezed lime juice, to garnish

Method:
1. Preheat the oven to 420°F.
2. Line a baking sheet with parchment paper.
3. Put the chopped cauliflower on the baking sheet, drizzle with 1 teaspoon of olive oil and sprinkle with sea salt.
4. Roast the cauliflower for 30-40 minutes, or until it is soft and starts to brown.
5. While the cauliflower is roasting, combine the rest of the soup.
6. Heat the remaining 2 teaspoons of olive oil in a large pot over medium-high heat.
7. Add the onion and sauté for 5 minutes.
8. Add the carrots and continue to cook, stirring occasionally, until carrots and onion are brown, about 10 minutes.
9. Add the ginger and garlic and cook for 1 minute.
10. Add the turmeric and Thai curry paste and cook for 1 more minute.
11. Deglaze the pan with ¼ cup vegetable stock.
12. Add the remaining stock and bring the pot to a boil. Reduce the heat to low and gently simmer until the cauliflower has finished cooking.
13. Pull the cauliflower from the oven and add it to the pot.
14. Using a blender puree the soup.
15. Pour, serve and enjoy!

Whole30 Tip:
Double this recipe and freeze what you do not use. It's easy to thaw and reheat for quick meals to take to work for lunch, or even for a mid day snack. The easier you make it to

eat healthier meals the more likely you will be to succeed. Need a little extra for lunch, or want to turn this into a dinner for the family? Make a spinach salad with some grilled chicken to go with it.

Bacon Wrapped Coconut Chicken Nuggets

"I unfortunately still crave chicken McNuggets and bacon, which is the meat candy of the world." – Katy Perry

Obviously Katy Perry hasn't tried this version of chicken nuggets yet. Delicious and much better for you then the processed shaped nuggets calling out to you from the drive through. Give it a try and serve it up to the pickiest eaters in your family. They won't be disappointed.

Serves: 2
Time: 10 minutes

Ingredients:
- 1 lb chicken strips
- 4 individual slices of bacon
- ¼ cup shredded coconut
- 1 tbsp coconut flour
- Salt and pepper to taste
- ¼ tsp garlic powder
- ¼ tsp paprika
- 1 tbsp dried parsley
- 2 tbsp coconut oil
- Skewers

Method:
1. Cut each chicken strip and each piece of bacon into 3 pieces.
2. In a bowl, combine shredded coconut, coconut flour, salt, pepper, garlic powder, paprika, and parsley.
3. Place chicken pieces in coconut coating, press and roll to get them to stick.
4. Wrap each piece of chicken piece with bacon.
5. Thread about 6 chicken pieces on a skewer.
6. Heat skillet to medium-high heat, add coconut oil and allow to heat.
7. Place skewers in skillet and cook, turning every 3 minutes, or until completely cooked.

Freeze For Later Directions:
After step 5 place the skewers in gallon freezer bags. After threading on skewers, place in gallon freezer bags. When you are ready to cook them defrost overnight in the fridge and continue with steps 6 and 7.

Artichoke Chicken Thighs

"I'm a thigh-meat dude. Thigh is just the best meat - I don't get chicken breast. I think it's a publicity stunt that we've convinced people it's delicious." – Patrice O'Neal

As children we used to fight over the thighs. Ending up with the breast meant you were to slow in our family. The moisture of the thigh adds a rich sweetness to the chicken better trapping in the many flavors added to this dish.

Serves: 2
Time: 30 minutes

Ingredients:
- 1 lb organic chicken thighs
- Salt and pepper to taste
- ½ tsp paprika
- ½ tsp onion powder
- ½ tsp dried parsley
- 1 tbsp avocado oil
- ¼ onion, chopped
- 1 cup mushrooms, chopped
- 1 clove garlic, diced
- ½ can artichoke hearts, quartered
- 1 tbsp capers
- ½ lemon, sliced

Method:
1. Heat a cast iron skillet over medium heat. Add in the avocado oil.
2. While the pan is heating, season the chicken thighs on each side with salt, pepper, paprika, onion powder and dried parsley.
3. Preheat your oven to 425°F.
4. Add the chicken to the skillet and cook for 5 minutes on each side.
5. Once the chicken has browned on each side, add all of the other ingredients except the lemon and mix together in the skillet.

6. Top the chicken with the sliced lemon.
7. Transfer the pan into the preheated oven to cook for 15 minutes.
8. Remove and let cool 5 minutes before serving.

Meatballs

"I wanted to be a skinny little ballerina but I was a voluptuous little Italian girl whose dad had meatballs on the table every night." – Lady Gaga

One of the best things about Whole30 is that there is no sacrifice on taste. You can still have the things you love, you can still be taken back to those childhood memories, you just have to be smart about how you recreate the dish.

Serves: 2
Time: 30 minutes

Ingredients:
- 1 lb grass-fed ground beef or ground turkey or a combination of both
- 1 egg, room temperature
- 1 tbsp Italian seasoning
- A pinch of salt
- ¼ cup almond flour
- 1 tbsp coconut aminos

Method:
1. Preheat the oven to 400°F and line a sheet tray with parchment paper.
2. In a large bowl, combine beef egg, Italian seasoning, salt, almond flour, and coconut aminos. With your hands mix until everything is completely combined.
3. Use a cookie scoop to make balls. Roll between palms to make smooth.
4. Place on prepared sheet tray and bake for 20 minutes.
5. Serve with tomato sauce or alone.

Tomato Basil Beef Soup

"Only the pure in heart can make a good soup." – Ludwig van Beethoven

Many nights growing up were spent with a mug of warm tomato soup in my hands. It was an inexpensive delicious meal and today the smell of it on the stove transports me immediately back to my childhood.

Serves 2
Total Time: 30 minutes

Ingredients:
- 15 oz tomatoes, fire roasted and diced
- ½ cup coconut milk
- 1 tsp coconut oil
- ½ cup onion, diced
- 2 tsp minced Garlic
- ½ tsp salt
- ½ cup chicken broth
- 2 tbsp fresh basil, chopped
- ¾ cups ground beef, cooked

Method:
1. Blend tomatoes and coconut milk in a blender until smooth.
2. Heat a large stockpot over medium-high heat.
3. Add coconut oil and sauté onions until translucent.
4. Add garlic and sauté.
5. Pour tomato/coconut milk mixture, salt and chicken broth into stockpot. Bring to a boil.
6. Reduce heat to simmer 10-15 minutes.
7. Mix in fresh basil and cooked ground beef. Cook until heated through.

Freeze For Later Directions:
1. Follow steps 1-7.
2. Let cool.
3. Divide mixture into indicated number of freezer bags. Label and freeze.
4. When ready to eat defrost and reheat in microwave for 2 minutes.

Buffalo Wings with Veggies

"All food is comfort food. Maybe I just like to chew." – Lewis Black

Chicken wings have been my comfort food since the first time they were introduced to me. A good bone in wing, I'm a strong believer that boneless wings are nothing more then chicken nuggets dripping with sauce is my comfort go-to. This dish is perfect for lunch or to make on game day to share with friends. Trust me, no one will know that this part of an elimination diet, you might even forget!

Serves: 2
Time: 1 hour 20 minutes

Ingredients:
- 1 lb chicken wings
- 1 ½ tsp baking powder
- ½ tsp sea salt
- 2 tbsp ghee or coconut oil
- ¼ cup Whole30 compliant hot sauce
- 1 ½ tsp apple cider vinegar
- ½ tsp garlic powder
- ¼ tsp paprika
- Pinch of cayenne pepper
- ½ tsp sea salt
- Carrots, jicama, and celery to slice

Method:
1. Preheat oven to 250°F. Line a large rimmed baking sheet with foil. Place a baking/cooling rackon the baking sheet and set aside.
2. Place chicken wins in a large bowl. Sprinkle with baking powder and sea salt. Toss well to coat.
3. Place chicken on the baking/cooking rack in a single layer. Wings should not touch.
4. Place pan in oven and cook chicken for 30 minutes.
5. After 30 minutes, turn the oven temperature to 425°F and cook for 20 minutes.
6. After 20 minutes, rotate the pan and cook another 20 minutes or until chicken is crispy and lightly browned.
7. While baking, prepare the sauce. Combine ghee, hot sauce, apple cider vinegar, garlic powder, paprika, cayenne pepper, and salt in a small saucepan over medium heat. Once ghee is melted, whisk and remove from heat.
8. Transfer cooked chicken wings to a shallow container and drizzle with 1/2 of the sauce. Toss to coat.
9. Serve wings with remaining sauce and sliced carrots, jicama, and celery.
10. Enjoy!

Dinner (Week 2 & 4)

Sautéed Cabbage and Potatoes

"At lunchtime, our kitchen was like a mini restaurant: my grandmother and mother had to cook for as many as 25 people - extended family plus 10 employees. We ate a lot of cabbage and a lot of potatoes." – Jean-Georges Vongerichten

This is a recipe you will want to hold onto long after you have completed the Whole30 challenge. It is an inexpensive delicious way to feed a crowd.

Serves: 4
Time: 1 hour 20 minutes

Ingredients:
- 8 red potatoes, peeled and sliced into matchsticks
- 2 ½ cups green cabbage, shredded
- 1 carrot, peeled & sliced
- 2 cloves garlic, minced
- 1 tsp dried thyme
- Salt, to taste
- 3 Roma tomatoes, sliced

Method:
1. Preheat the oven to 350°F.
2. Toss potatoes, cabbage, carrot & garlic in a baking dish.
3. Season with thyme and salt.
4. Lay slices of tomato across the top. Cover the dish with a layer of foil and place in the preheated oven.
5. Bake for 35 minutes. Remove and discard the foil. Toss gently and cook for another 30 minutes or until potatoes are browned and tender.
6. Enjoy!

Whole30 Tip:
If this dish is to light for you and you need a protein simply season and bake a piece of chicken in a separate dish at the same time. Use the same herbs: thyme, garlic, and salt with a little pepper added in. By this point in the journey you should know what will and won't satisfy you. Adjust your meals accordingly.

Salmon with Prosciutto Wrapped Asparagus

"Good asparagus needs minimal treatment and is best eaten with few other ingredients." – Yotam Ottolenghi

Salmon and asparagus are two of my favorites. Both are simply prepared and complement each other well. The key to each is freshness. The best meals are straight from the pond and the garden. Choose the quality of your ingredients wisely and your palette will thank you.

Serves: 4
Time: 40 minutes

Ingredients:
- 2 lb salmon
- Coconut oil spray
- ½ tsp salt
- ½ tsp pepper
- ½ tsp onion powder
- ½ tsp garlic powder
- 1 lemon, sliced

Method:
1. Preheat oven to 400°F.
2. Line a baking sheet with foil and spray with cooking spray. Place salmon on foil and spray with cooking spray.
3. Sprinkle salt, pepper, onion powder, garlic powder, and lemon slices on salmon.
4. Wrap salmon in foil and bake for 18 to 20 minutes or until salmon flakes easily with a fork.
5. While salmon is cooking prepare asparagus.

Prosciutto Wrapped Asparagus

Ingredients:
- 1 lb asparagus, tough ends cut away (try to get thicker asparagus, not pencil thin)
- 6 oz prosciutto
- Coconut oil spray
- ½ cup mayonnaise (Whole30 compliant)
- Zest from 2 lemons, about 1 tbsp
- 2 garlic clove, very finely minced

Method:
1. Cut each piece of prosciutto in half lengthwise.
2. Wrap each piece of asparagus with 1 of the half slices of prosciutto. Begin at the bottom, and wrap at an upward angle.
3. Repeat until all the asparagus is wrapped.
4. Set in the fridge while you prepare the lemon garlic aioli.
5. In a small mixing bowl, combine the mayo, lemon zest and garlic. Stir until combined.
6. Refrigerate until ready to serve.
7. After the salmon is done cooking raise the oven temperature to 450°F. Move the oven rack to the top of the oven.
8. Line a baking sheet with parchment paper (not necessary, but makes for easier cleanup).
9. Arrange the prosciutto wrapped asparagus in a single layer. Spray with olive oil spray.
10. Roast in the oven for about 10 minutes, until the prosciutto is crispy, turning the asparagus halfway thru.
11. Serve warm or at room temperature with the lemon garlic aioli.

Chicken and Roasted Veggies

"All great change in America begins at the dinner table." – Ronald Reagan

All great change in general begins at the dinner table. It's where we teach our children values, where we discuss the world with friends, where we share food and drink and hospitality. Memories are made here. The choices you are making today for yourself will impact your own life but also the lives of those around you. Remember the inspiration you are and keep pushing forward. You've come this far! You can make it!

Serves: 4
Time: 30 minutes

Ingredients:
- ¼ cup date paste
- ¼ cup coconut aminos
- 2 tbsp brown mustard
- ¼ tsp onion powder
- ¼ tsp garlic powder
- ¼ tsp paprika

- Pinch of black pepper
- 2 lb boneless skinless chicken thighs
- 1 sweet potato, chopped into ½ inch pieces
- 1 med red bell pepper, cut into 1 inch pieces
- 1 med purple onion, cut into quarters
- 1 med broccoli crown, cut into florets about 1 ½ cups florets
- 3 tbsp cooking fat for roasting veggies divided
- Salt and black pepper to taste

Method:
1. Preheat your oven to 450°F.
2. In a blender add the date paste, coconut aminos, brown mustard, onion powder, garlic powder, paprika, and black pepper. Blend until combined.
3. Line two baking sheets with foil.
4. Coat chicken on both sides with the sauce and arrange on foil lined baking sheet
5. Toss potatoes with 1/2 tbsp cooking fat and sprinkle with salt and black pepper.
6. Arrange in single layer on second baking sheet, separate from chicken
7. Roast the chicken and potatoes in the preheated oven for 10 minutes. Toss the remaining veggies with remaining cooking fat and sprinkle with salt and pepper to taste
8. After 10 minutes, add these veggies to the baking sheet with potatoes. Return to oven (near bottom) to roast 10-15 more minutes, turn\ chicken once to evenly cook and stir the veggies and potatoes.
9. Put under the broiler for last 2-5 minutes or so to brown chicken and veggies.
10. Serve and enjoy!

Whole30 Tip:

A reminder, some ingredients for the Whole30 may be difficult to come by. Date paste was used in the grilled pineapple recipe on week 1. If you purchased date paste you should still have plenty. If not here is the reminder of how to make your own.

*To make date paste, blend 1/3 cup dates (softened first in hot water if too dry) with 2 Tbsp water in a high speed blender until pureed. Add drops of water as needed to create a smooth consistency.

Pumpkin Chili

"Every December, I host a tree-trimming party. I serve chili with cornbread and lots of good wine. It's a wonderful party, and it shows how much adults like to play." – Maya Angelou

Maybe skip the cornbread and serve the pumpkin biscuits (you'll find them in the holiday guide) instead. Put out the wine for the guests. Host a pumpkin carving party for halloween, a chili cookoff, or a tree-trimming party like Maya Angelou. Food is a wonderful place to gather around. Participating in the Whole30 is about eliminating certain foods, not friends and fellowship. You aren't skipping out on life or social events. You are learning self-discipline in the midst of it all.

Serves: ALOT

Time: Sits on stove top all day. Start in the morning. The longer it simmers the richer the flavors.

Ingredients:
- 1/3 cup chili powder
- 2 tsp smoked paprika
- 1 tsp ground cumin
- 1 tsp turmeric
- 2 tbsp coconut oil (or drippings from the meat)
- 1 lb ground beef
- 1 lb ground chicken
- 1 lb ground pork
- 2 large onions, chopped and divided (3/4 + 1/4)
- 1 large bell pepper, chopped
- 2 jalapeños seeded and diced (if the flesh is too spicy, only use one!)
- 3 large cloves garlic, minced
- 2 (28 oz) cans crushed tomatoes
- 2 cups pumpkin purée
- Salt & pepper
- 2 tbsp Chipotle in adobo sauce

Method:
1. In a bowl, stir together chili powder, smoked paprika, cumin, and turmeric.
2. In a large 4-6 quart pot or dutch oven, over medium high heat, brown the ground beef seasoning with a large spoonful of the spice blend. Remove to a plate.
3. Brown the ground pork seasoning with a large spoonful of the spice blend. Remove to a large plate.
4. Brown the ground chicken (or turkey) seasoning with a large spoonful of the spice blend. Remove to a large plate.
5. Keep 2 tbsp of the oil from the meat in the pan, drain off the rest. If you do not have 2 tbsp of fat drippings add coconut oil to the pan.

6. Stir 3/4 of the chopped onions, the bell peppers and the jalapeños into the hot oil or grease in the pot. Season with a large spoonful of the seasoning, and salt & pepper. Sauté until tender and starting to brown. Stir in the garlic and let cook for about 30 seconds, until very fragrant, before adding back in the 3 meats. Do not drain the meat, add the drippings with the meat. Add the crushed tomatoes and the pumpkin.
7. Stir well, scraping the bottom of the pan with a wooden spoon to get up any good bits on the bottom, and add in the rest of the seasoning mixture. Stir well to combine, bring to a boil and then reduce the heat to low. Simmer all day.
8. Before serving taste for seasoning and add more salt & pepper as needed. If it's not spicy enough for you add chipotle.
9. Stir in the remaining chopped onions.
10. Enjoy! Don't eat it all. Save some for tomorrow's loaded baked potatoes.

Loaded Baked Potatoes

"Leftovers in their less visible form are called memories. Stored in the refrigerator of the mind and the cupboard of the heart." – Thomas Fuller

Baked potatoes are a great conduit for leftovers. Bake up a variety of potatoes, or just one kind. Put out a spread of the leftovers from the fridge. Add a bowl of steamed broccoli to make sure there's a vegetable and you have a fun baked potato bar where everyone can customize their own dinner. They are both fun and a great way to reduce food waste in your home.

Serves: 4
Time: 1 hour

Ingredients:

- 2 sweet potatoes
- 2 russet potatoes
- 4 strips bacon, cooked and chopped
- ¼ cup scallions, chopped
- 4 tbsp ghee
- 2 tbsp avocado or coconut oil
- Pumpkin Chili
- ¼ cup steamed broccoli florets

Method:

1. Preheat oven to 400°F.
2. Rub all potatoes with oil of choice and place on rack of oven, allow 45 minutes to cook or until tender when poked with a fork.
3. When potatoes are finished cooking, allow 5 minutes to cool then split open in halves.
4. Add 1 tbsp of ghee to each potato.
5. Spoon pumpkin chili and steamed broccoli over each potato. Garnish with bacon and scallions.
6. Enjoy!

Spicy Beef and Broccoli

"Broccoli is incredible. It can prevent DNA damage and metastatic cancer spread; activate defences against pathogens and pollutants; help to prevent lymphoma; boost the enzymes that detox your liver; target breast cancer stem cells; and reduce the risk of prostate cancer progression." – Michael Greger

Broccoli is versatile and goes great with any meal. It's a great go to side for any meal but even better when incorporated into the dish. It picks up the richness of the flank steak and the sweetness from the pineapple juice. This will become a family favorite for sure.

Serves: 4
Time: 2 hours 10 minutes

Ingredients:
- 2 tbsp coconut aminos
- ½ tsp garlic powder
- ½ tsp onion powder
- 2 tbsp coconut oil
- 3 tbsp pineapple juice
- 1 lb flank steak
- 2 cups broccoli florets, fresh or frozen
- 1 tsp red pepper flakes

Method:
1. In a bowl, combine first 5 ingredients.
2. Marinate steak and broccoli in sauce for at least 2 hours. Can be marinated and stored in the refrigerator overnight.

3. Dump marinade, broccoli, and steak into a skillet and cook over medium heat for approximately 4 minutes.
4. Add red pepper flakes and cook for 2 more minutes.
5. Serve and enjoy!

Pulled Pork Shoulder with Turnips

"On some subconscious level, I've been prejudiced against turnips, parsnips, swedes and other roots. Do they taste of much? Are they really special? How wrong I was." – Yotam Ottolenghi

Confession. I always double this recipe and put an extra one in the freezer for later. This is a great dish to have during the reintroduction phase of Whole30. Just add a nice crusty loaf of bread for the night you reintroduce bread. Make it now and save it for up to a month. The house smells amazing while it cooks. I was hesitant to try turnips at first, like Ottolenghi I had my prejudices. But I was wrong. They add a natural sweetness to the pork and the dish is dull without them.

Serves 4
Total Time: 2 hours 10 minutes

Ingredients
- 2 lbs Pork Roast
- 1 garlic clove cut into thin slices
- 1/3 tsp salt
- ¾ to 1 lb baby turnips
- 2 cups diced fresh broccoli

Instructions
1. Cut small slits in the roast.
2. Press a sliver of garlic into each slit and salt pork roast all over.
3. Place roast in the slow cooker and cook on high for 4 hours.
4. Add turnips and continue to cook for 60 minutes or longer on low, until they soften.
5. Add broccoli and cook for 20 minutes on low.
6. Scoop into bowls and enjoy!

Chapter 10: Holiday Tips & Encouragement

Holiday Tips & Encouragement

One of the most difficult parts of eating Whole30 is the holidays. There are so many tempting foods, especially when it comes to sweets. Thanksgiving and Christmas can easily become your excuse to put this important program to the side for another few months.

Do not let that happen.

There is never a better time than now to begin.

With careful planning and dedication you can successfully complete the Whole30 diet without sacrificing quality family time around the table.

Here are a few tips and recipes to help you plan for these two holidays centered around feasting.

TIPS

- How to avoid alcohol. Have sparkling water on hand for toasts. La Croix is a delicious brand with a variety of flavors and no added sugar. Add a twist of citrus and ice to your glass and no one will even know you are alcohol free for the evening. (This is also an excellent tip for business trips and late-night networking at the hotel bar). If this doesn't work simply offer to be the designated driver for the evening. You'll have an excuse and be helping your friends at the same time.

- How to avoid sugar. Skip the sweets. It's really that simple. If you start ahead of time by the time the day gets here, you will have lost your taste for them anyway. Don't believe me? Allow yourself one tiny nibble, I promise it will satiate you. The sweetness will be overpowering and you'll be shocked how you were ever able to eat half of grandma's apple pie every year prior.

- What to eat. Stick to the turkey, ham, and green vegetables. Volunteer to bring the sweet potatoes or a salad as a side. There are some great sides included in this guide. Other's will be so involved in their own food they won't even notice what you have and haven't put on your plate. Avoid talking about your diet and no one will pressure you to break it.

- Offer to host the meal and encourage your guests to each bring their favorites to add to the below menu that you will be preparing. You may not be able to try theirs but at least you will have enough of your favorites to not be tempted. The best news is they won't be deprived of their holiday favorites either!

Of course, if you are the host then there is a number of wonderful recipes your guests will enjoy and will keep you Whole30 compliant. You don't have to sacrifice the comfort foods of your holidays to stay on your diet. Food is meant to be enjoyed, so let's enjoy it! The main course for your holiday meal is simple. Healthy grass-fed organic meats and free range poultry are all allowed. The good news is that if you are stuck at a friend's for the Holidays who isn't Whole30 you can always eat a plate of turkey (that is if it isn't fried) and stick to the veggie tray and nutrition dense options. Maybe stock your pockets with a few almonds to help.

This year why not try a Turducken. That's a turkey stuffed with duck stuffed with chicken. It's a delicious experience during the holidays. You can find them at a Whole Foods or local grocery store during the holidays. With this on the table your plate won't have room for all the delicious sides!

In Week 1 & 3 see the recipe for Roasted Turkey and Root Vegetables. It's the main course and side all in one. The Mint Lamb Chops would be a great addition to any Christmas or Easter celebration as well. Simply increase the recipes to fit the number of servings.

Whole30 deserts aren't allowed, no room for cheating right? Wrong. It's the holidays! Live a little through your pallet. We're not asking you to break the no sugar code but it's going to be a full year before Christmas cookies are offered to you again. You can replace the apple pie with warm cinnamon apples and the pumpkin pie with the pumpkin pudding found in week 1 & 3.

Here's the thing. Holiday foods are special and before you pass up the memories of a Christmas cookie or grandma's pecan pie be sure to weigh the connection these foods bring you to others. What is the emotional significance of the food? Don't offend grandma but do be aware of the amount of sugar and non-compliant whole30 foods you are eating. Make a conscious choice and then don't beat yourself over it. January is a month for all of us to regroup and restart.

Enjoy your holidays. Drink some eggnog and toast in the New Year. Be aware of your food choices. It isn't cheating if it is a conscious choice for fellowship and heritage over elimination.

Your relationship with food is changing, not your relationships with people.

The best recommendation is to plan your Whole30 with plenty of time to reintroduce foods before the holidays so that you know whether or not that apple pie is worth eating or if you'd be better off skipping the wine and cheese. If you can't get a full 37 days (Whole30 plus reintroduction) in before the holidays then wait till after. If you are set on doing this now, it is doable and this menu will help. Just be aware that the temptation will be greater. If you don't think that you can pass up the green bean casserole this year then simply wait till you are better able to be successful.

If you are determined here are a few sides to add to your holiday feast and organic free range turkey.

Each recipe serves 10. Decrease or increase based on the size of your party. Recipes follow.

Caramelized Brussel Sprouts / Sweet Potato Casserole / Stuffing / Pumpkin Butter Biscuit / Cranberry Sauce

Chapter 11: Holiday Side Dishes

Caramelized Brussel Sprouts

Serves: 10
Time: 55 minutes

Brussel sprouts are a delicious green dish to add to the Thanksgiving and Christmas table. The duck fat gives them richness while the pecans transform them into a holiday dish.

Ingredients:
- 2 lb Brussels Sprouts, halved
- 1 medium onion, chopped
- 4 cloves garlic, minced
- ½ cup fat (duck fat is my favorite for this recipe)
- 2 tbsp fresh thyme, minced
- 1 cup pecans, chopped
- Salt and pepper to taste
- Lemon juice

Method:
1. Preheat oven to 425 °F.
2. Combine Brussels sprouts, onion, and garlic in a bowl and coat with the duck fat.
3. Add thyme, salt, & pepper. Toss to coat.
4. Spread on a foil wrapped baking sheet (with a lipped edge) for 20 minutes. Sprinkle chopped pecans over the Brussels sprouts and cook for another 10 minutes or until sprouts feel tender and cooked through.
5. Squeeze fresh lemon juice over the sprouts and serve.

Sweet Potato Casserole

Serves: 10
Time: 55 minutes

No holiday feast is complete without a sweet potato casserole. On Whole 30 there's no debate between marshmallows or pecan topping. Topped with walnuts and cinnamon you'll never question the correct topping again.

Ingredients:
- 15 large sweet potatoes, peeled and diced
- 3 crisp apples, peeled and diced
- 2 ½ cups walnuts, finely chopped
- 1 ¼ cup full-fat coconut milk
- 3 tbsp vanilla extract
- 2 tbsp cinnamon
- 2 tbsp nutmeg
- 6 tbsp real butter
- Salt & pepper to taste

Method:
1. Preheat oven to 350F.
2. Place sweet potatoes and apples in a large pot. Fill with water, completely covering potatoes and apples, and bring to a boil over high-heat. Boil for 15 to 20 minutes until potatoes are tender.
3. Remove from heat and strain.
4. Return potatoes and apples to the pan, drizzle 2 tbsp melted butter on top.
5. Using a masher or hand-mixer, mash until smooth.
6. As you mash slowly pour in the coconut milk. Depending on your preference adjust the milk to your level of creaminess.
7. Add the vanilla extract. Salt & pepper to taste.

8. Place the mash in a casserole dish and set to the side.
9. In a medium bowl, toss walnuts with remaining butter, cinnamon, and nutmeg.
10. Evenly cover the mashed potato mixture with the spiced walnuts.
11. Place in preheated oven and cook for 20 minutes. Enjoy!

Stuffing

Serves: 10
Time: 1 hour and 20 minutes

Whole30 does not mean you have to sacrifice the stuffing on Thanksgiving. It just means you have to get creative. This grain-free alternative has all you need to satisfy your stuffing craving.

Ingredients:
- 4 onions, diced
- 1 bunch celery, diced
- 5 apples, diced
- 2 pears, diced
- 1 ¼ cup combination of chopped dates, raisins, and/or cranberries
- 5 cups almond flour
- 3 tbsp sage
- 3 tbsp thyme
- 1 tsp rosemary
- 1 tsp pepper
- 2 tsp salt
- 1/4 cup duck fat
- 7 eggs, whisked

Method:
1. Preheat oven to 350F
2. Grease large baking dish.
3. Add ¼ cup duck fat to a large saucepan and heat over low/med heat.
4. Add onion, celery, apple, pears, and herbs. Sauté over medium heat for 5 minutes and remove from heat. Pour into baking dish.
5. In a bowl combine almond flour, dates, raisins, and cranberries. Add the lightly beaten eggs and mix well.
6. Spoon the mixture over the onions, celery, apple, pears, and herbs.
7. Bake at 350F for 1 hour.

Pumpkin Butter Biscuit

Serves: 10
Time: 20 minutes

This savory biscuit is ideal to serve alongside your Holiday feast. For those joining you that are not on the Whole30 diet simply put out a package of premade dinner rolls. At the end of the night we're certain the pumpkin butter biscuits will have one over even the most skeptical and the others will be added to the take home boxes.

Ingredients:
- 3 cups almond flour
- 1/3 cup coconut flour
- 1 ½ cup arrowroot powder
- 3 tsp baking powder
- 1 tsp salt
- ½ tsp pumpkin pie spice
- ¾ cup canned pumpkin
- 3 eggs
- ½ cup real butter, room temperature

Method:
1. Preheat oven to 350F.
2. Combine dry ingredients in a bowl.
3. Combine wet ingredients in a different bowl and slowly combine.
4. Line a baking sheet with parchment paper.
5. Roll dough into balls.
6. Bake for 12 minutes, cooked through and flakey.
7. Serve with real butter or cream cheese and honey.

Cranberry Sauce

Serves: 10
Time: 1 hour

Cranberry sauce without added sugar is difficult to come by. If you find some, buy it in bulk for the holiday, but in case you don't, here is a recipe perfect for your holiday table.

Ingredients:
- 8 cups apple cider
- 1 tsp whole cloves
- 1 tsp dried orange peel
- 2 cinnamon sticks
- 6 cups cranberries
- 6 medjool dates, pitted and minced
- ¼ tsp vanilla

Method:
1. Place cider and spices in a large saucepan. Put the cloves and orange peel in a spice bag and place in saucepan as well.
2. Bring to a boil over medium high heat and let reduce for 20-30 minutes. It should reduce down to half.
3. Remove the spice bag and add cranberries, dates, and vanilla. Simmer for 20 more minutes.
4. Transfer to a blender and puree until smooth.

Chapter 12: You Did It!

You Did It!

If you've made it this far it's because you have completed the 30 Day Whole Food Challenge.

Congratulations!

You have proven to the most important person, YOU, that you are capable of doing amazing things. You have set your mind on a goal and you have reached it.

Remember this is more than a 30 day challenge. It is a lifestyle change. Today you know more about your own body, your own challenges, and your own health then you did before you began. Today is when you take control of your own health and wellness. Today is when you begin to make the best possible choices and are able to use the knowledge you gained to control food choices rather than allow them to control you.

Chapter 13: Measurements & Equivalents

Measurements & Equivalents
- a dash = 8 drops (liquid) ≈ ⅛ teaspoon (slightly less)
- 1 teaspoon = 60 drops
- 3 teaspoons = 1 tablespoon = ½ fluid ounce
- ½ tablespoon = 1½ teaspoons
- 2 tablespoons (liquid) = 1 fluid ounce = ⅛ cup
- 3 tablespoons = 1 ½ fluid ounces = 1 jigger
- 4 tablespoons = ¼ cup
- ⅛ cup = 2 tablespoons
- ⅙ cup = 2 tablespoons + 2 teaspoons
- ⅓ cup = 5 tablespoons + 1 teaspoon
- 1 cup = ½ pint = 8 fluid ounces
- 2 cups = 1 pint = 16 fluid ounces
- 4 cups = 1 quart = 2 pints = 32 fluid ounces
- 4 quarts = 1 gallon
- 1 peck = 8 quarts = 2 gallons
- 1 bushel = 4 pecks

Chapter 14: UK to US conversions

Use this helpful guide to find baking and cooking conversions between metric, imperial and US cup measures. This will also help you in adjusting recipes to your prepared servings.

Volume
When measuring liquid, cooking measurements are quite straightforward:

Metric   Imperial   US cups
- 250ml 8 fl oz   1 cup
- 180ml 6 fl oz   3/4 cup
- 150ml 5 fl oz   2/3 cup
- 120ml 4 fl oz   1/2 cup
- 75ml   2 1/2 fl oz   1/3 cup
- 60ml   2 fl oz   1/4 cup
- 30ml   1 fl oz   1/8 cup
- 15ml   1/2 fl oz   1 tablespoon

Weight

UK to US conversions

Imperial   Metric
- ½ oz   15g
- 1 oz   30g
- 2 oz   60g
- 3 oz   90g
- 4 oz   110g
- 5 oz   140g
- 6 oz   170g
- 7 oz   200g
- 8 oz   225g
- 9 oz   255g
- 10 oz   280g
- 11 oz   310g
- 12 oz   340g
- 13 oz   370g
- 14 oz   400g
- 15 oz   425g
- 1 lb   450g

- 3 teaspoons = 1 tablespoon
- 1 teaspoon   5ml
- 2 teaspoons   10ml
- 1 tablespoon 15ml
- 2 tablespoons   30ml
- 3 tablespoons   45ml
- 4 tablespoons   60ml
- 5 tablespoons   75ml
- 6 tablespoons   90ml
- 7 tablespoons   105ml

Tablespoons to US cups
- 1 tablespoon 1/16 cup
- 2 tablespoons   1/8 cup
- 4 tablespoons   1/4 cup
- 5 tablespoons   1/3 cup

- 8 tablespoons   1/2 cup
- 10 tablespoons   2/3 cup
- 12 tablespoons   3/4 cup
- 16 tablespoons   1 cup

Printed by
Libri Plureos GmbH · Friedensallee 273
22763 Hamburg · Germany